REAL JUSTICE:

CONVICTED FOR BEING MI'KMAQ

• • •

THE STORY OF DONALD MARSHALL JR.

BILL SWAN

LORIMER

JAMES LORIMER & COMPANY LTD., PUBLISHERS
TORONTO

James Lorimer & Company Ltd., Publishers acknowledges the support of the Ontario Arts Council. We acknowledge the financial support of the Government of Canada through the Canada Book Fund for our publishing activities. We acknowledge the support of the Canada Council for the Arts which last year invested $24.3 million in writing and publishing throughout Canada. We acknowledge the Government of Ontario through the Ontario Media Development Corporation's Ontario Book Initiative.

ONTARIO ARTS COUNCIL
CONSEIL DES ARTS DE L'ONTARIO

Canada Council
for the Arts

Cover image: © 2009 Canadian Press Images

Library and Archives Canada Cataloguing in Publication

Swan, Bill, 1939-
    Real justice : convicted for being Mi'kmaq : the story of Donald Marshall Jr. / Bill Swan.

Includes index.
Issued also in electronic format.
ISBN 978-1-4594-0438-0 (bound).--ISBN 978-1-4594-0439-7 (pbk.)

    1. Marshall, Donald, 1953-. 2. Murder--Nova Scotia--Sydney--Case studies. 3. Trials (Murder)--Nova Scotia--Sydney--Case studies. 4. Racism--Nova Scotia--Sydney--Case studies. 5. Judicial error--Nova Scotia--Sydney--Case studies. 6. False imprisonment--Canada--Case studies. I. Title.

HV6535.C32N64 2013   364.152'30971695   C2013-900108-5

James Lorimer & Company Ltd.,
Publishers
317 Adelaide Street West, Suite 1002
Toronto, ON, Canada
M5V 1P9
www.lorimer.ca

Distributed in the United States by:
Orca Book Publishers
P.O. Box 468
Custer, WA, USA
98240-0468

Printed and bound in Canada
Manufactured by Friesens Corporation in Altona, Manitoba, Canada in February 2013
Job #81644

FOR KATHY

"Donald Marshall Jr. was convicted and sent to prison, in part at least, because he was a Native person."
— Royal Commission on the Donald Marshall Jr.,
Prosecution.

CONTENTS

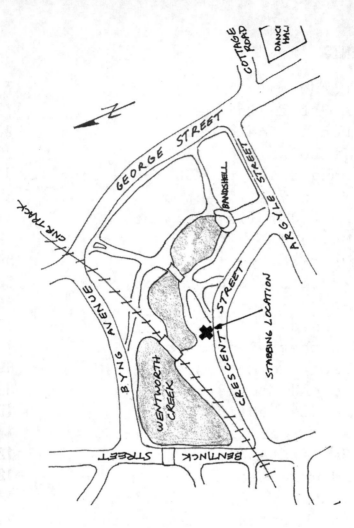

Map created by Daniel Mansfield

NOTE

The dialogue in this book is taken for the most part directly from transcripts of hearings and from statements given by witnesses. Some latitude has been taken to create a narrative flow to the story, but on all key points of testimony the quoted material is from official documents.

FOREWORD

The story of Donald Marshall Jr.'s wrongful conviction is a story of courage and betrayal, of perseverance and luck. Surviving the ordeal of eleven years of wrongful imprisonment — described by many wrongfully convicted persons as the equivalent of being buried alive — required Donald Marshall to draw on depths of strength he had no reason to know he possessed. Eleven years of struggle to survive the harsh realities of prison and then eight more years after his release before being exonerated by the Royal Commission of Inquiry that examined how the criminal justice system had betrayed him.

The Royal Commission's 1990 report was a searing indictment of the system of justice that wrongfully convicted an innocent seventeen-year-old in 1971 and kept him locked up while he grew into adulthood. Wrongful conviction robbed Donald Marshall of far more than just his liberty. The eldest son of the Grand Chief of the Mi'kmaw Nation, Donald Marshall was deprived of the kinship of his large, close-knit family and community; separated from his language and culture; and subjected to the daily tensions, humiliations, and violence of prison life. His existence was one of survival and struggle, long after he walked out through the prison gates.

When Donald Marshall was released from prison in 1982, freed on bail following the reopening of his case, he faced the ordeal of trying to establish his innocence. Although acquitted in 1983 of the murder of Sandy Seale, the victory was a bitter one: the Supreme Court of Nova Scotia (Appeal Division) laid responsibility for his wrongful conviction at his feet. Only the painstaking work of the Royal Commission of Inquiry finally exonerated him, finding that it was the legal system that had failed Mr. Marshall at virtually every turn.

The Royal Commission came to the painful conclusion that racism played a significant role in Mr. Marshall's wrongful arrest and conviction. Had Mr. Marshall been "White," the Commissioners found, the investigation by the Sydney police "would have taken a different course." The Commissioners concluded that Donald Marshall was "convicted and sent to prison, in part at least, because he was a Native person" describing the evidence supporting this "inescapable conclusion" as "persuasive". They characterized their determination that racism played a role in Mr. Marshall's imprisonment as "one of the most difficult and disturbing findings this Royal Commission has made."

The reality that factors such as race and socio-economic status contribute to making a person more vulnerable to being wrongfully convicted is deeply troubling. Indeed, as Donald Marshall's story reveals, his Aboriginal status made him vulnerable to being a victim in the very attack that killed Sandy Seale, who was himself a racialized person. It took the complete failure of the criminal justice system in Donald Marshall's case to transform him from the genuine victim of a racist attack to the falsely accused perpetrator of the crime.

Donald Marshall Jr.'s wrongful conviction was exposed at a time when Canadians and the Canadian criminal justice system had not yet confronted the extent to which the factors in his case, and those unique to subsequent cases, had operated to send other innocent people to prison for murders they did not commit. The wrongful convictions of David Milgaard, Guy Paul Morin, Thomas Sophonow, Gregory Parsons, Randy Druken, Ronald Dalton, James Driskell, William Mullins-Johnson and Steven Truscott were also eventually overturned with Royal Commissions or Courts of Appeal exhuming the errors that led to these men being buried alive by a flawed justice system. And this list is not exhaustive. With its legacy of wrongful convictions, the Canadian criminal justice system cannot afford to be complacent. Not only do wrongful convictions inflict a terrible toll on the innocent and their families, and ultimately on public confidence in the criminal justice system, but the broader community also remains at risk when the wrong person is locked away. It is a chilling fact that through all the years Mr. Marshall watched his life pass by in prison, Sandy Seale's killer was free in the community.

Donald Marshall Jr. was eventually compensated for his wrongful conviction by the Province of Nova Scotia, accepting the recommendations of a Royal Commission of Inquiry that examined the issue. His parents also received a small amount of compensation for their losses. All those years of travelling to visit their bewildered, angry son in prison. Raising their family without their first-born. Donald Marshall Jr.'s brothers and sisters growing up without him. The stigma of having a child convicted of murder. The agony of knowing he was innocent.

So much time has passed since Sandy Seale's murder in May 1971 — a tragedy that set into motion the awful forces that saw another young man lose a significant part of his life — that many Canadians have forgotten or do not know Mr. Marshall's harrowing story. Mr. Marshall, of course, did not have the luxury of forgetting what was done to him. He could never forget. No amount of compensation could have given him back what was taken from him by a justice system that was ready to believe, and to keep believing, that he was a killer. Donald Marshall's story is not just a cautionary tale about the criminal justice system, however, and how it can and must be improved; it is also a story of grit and integrity, of not giving up, of not losing all hope. It is a story of strength and spirit, of personal and cultural endurance, of the ultimate triumph of truth over lies. It is a story that Canadians should commit to memory. A story that can challenge and inspire. A story that tells us it is vital to believe, as Donald Marshall believed, that no matter what adversity we confront as individuals or more broadly as a society, we must not give up, even in the face of seemingly insurmountable odds.

— *Anne S. Derrick*

Derrick was one of Marshalls counsel at the Royal Commission of Inquiry on his prosecution; counsel to Marshall at the inquiry concerning the adequacy of compensation paid to him; and counsel (with Professor Archie Kaiser) to Marshall before the 1990 Inquiry Committee of the Canadian Judicial Council examining the conduct of the judges who sat on the 1982 Appeal Reference into Marshall's murder conviction. She is now a judge of the Provincial Court of Nova Scotia.

CHAPTER ONE

A STROLL IN THE PARK

MAY 28, 1971

Donald Marshall Jr. pulled on a cigarette and scuffed his toes into the bare ground at Wentworth Park.

Crappy night, he thought.

First, he had missed the dance. He was late returning from Halifax. By the time he arrived at the St. Joseph's Church hall, the dance was sold out. When you're seventeen and live in a place like Sydney, Nova Scotia, where not much ever happens, missing a dance is a big deal.

At just over six feet, with an athletic build, Donald moved like someone confident in his good looks. When he couldn't get into the dance, he hung around, looking for someone he knew. There would always be somebody.

He headed up the street towards Wentworth Park by the bandshell. A black youth dressed in bib overalls and a brown jacket walked by. It was Sandy Seale: a good-looking, friendly guy. Athletic, he played rep hockey and had been named a tournament MVP the previous year in a tournament in Ontario. He was Donald's age: seventeen.

Sandy wasn't a close buddy, but the year before Donald had helped his father drywall the Seale house. During breaks in the work, he and Sandy had played road hockey. Between them, they represented the two main groups of visible minorities in Sydney: Mi'kmaq and blacks.

"How's it goin', eh?" Donald asked.

Sandy shrugged. "Guess we missed the fight, Junior," Sandy said, calling Donald by the name most common with his chums. Earlier, a scuffle had broken out in the dance hall. It didn't last long. Police officers on the scene made sure of that.

"Tough," Donald replied. "The only excitement for the whole evening."

"Yeah," said Sandy.

"Who was in it?" Donald asked.

Sandy pointed to a couple who sat smoking on a nearby park bench. "Ask him," he said. "That's one of them over there."

Donald looked over. *Terry Gushue. And the girl, what was her name? Harriss. Patricia Harriss. What, fourteen? Kind of pretty; a bit young, though. But she looked angry.*

Sandy walked over to the couple on the bench. Donald followed. "Everything okay?" Donald asked.

Terry Gushue looked up through bloodshot eyes. "A fight started at the dance," Patricia said. "Terry got mixed up in it. He got kicked out."

She pulled on a cigarette, trying to look older than her age.

"All I wanted to do was dance," she said.

Yeah, thought Donald. From the hall, the song washed over the park: "Raindrops Keep Fallin' on My Head."

Donald thought that was funny.

Raindrops. Right.

The music from the church hall changed. "Bridge Over Troubled Waters."

"See?" said Patricia to Terry. "They're slowing the music down. The dance is almost over. We should be in there for the last dance."

"Well, they won't let me back in, will they?" replied Terry.

Nearby, at the edge of the park pavilion, another guy was on his hands and knees puking.

"We should see if he's okay," said Sandy.

Donald and Sandy walked over. Donald recognized him: Bobby Patterson.

"Had a bit too much, did you?" Sandy asked.

"Yeah, yeah," came the reply, the voice slurred. He looked pale.

"You know who we are?" asked Donald. *The guy was high, that's for sure. Bad business, mixing booze and drugs.* "What are our names?"

Bobby barfed again into the flower bed. "Hmm, oh, shit, I'm wasted. Yeah. Sandy, oh, crap, Seale. Donald Marshall." The names were right even if his pronunciation was heavily slurred

"Okay," said Donald, "but I think you better sit down for a while. Take it easy." He led the youth to the bandshell and helped tuck him behind a shrub.

"Stay there a bit," Donald said. "Don't let the cops find you or you'll spend the night in jail."

Retching muffled Bobby's thanks.

To their left, over Wentworth Creek which ran through the park, an older man waved them over. He wore a long, dark raincoat draped over his shoulders. He had white hair. With him was a younger man, too old to be a teenager. You didn't have to smell them to know they were drunk.

From the park bench, Patricia said, "They tried to bum a cigarette off us."

Sandy shrugged. "Well, we'll see what they want, and then I gotta catch my bus home." He headed towards the footbridge over the pond to see what the two men wanted.

Donald offered Terry Gushue a light.

"They're crazy," Patricia said.

"Likely drunk, too," said Donald. He turned to join Sandy over by the two men. "See ya," he said.

As he got nearer, the older of the two men, heavy set, maybe in his fifties, got louder, his words slurred. "Got a smoke, buddy?" he said. "We need a smoke."

"You're in right good shape, old man," Donald said.

The second man, mid-twenties maybe, thin, clean-shaven, said nothing. He wore a bulky, blue sweater and stood there, weaving, a silly drunken grin on his face.

"Give us a couple of smokes," said the old guy. His name was Roy Ebsary.

Donald looked at Ebsary. The older man wore his raincoat like a priest's cape. "You guys priests or something?" he asked,

Ebsary nodded. "We are, we are."

"Never seen you before," said Donald. "Where are you from?"

"Manitoba," the man replied. "So how 'bout a coupl'a smokes for men of the cloth?"

Donald smirked. *Priests, eh? Drunk in the park on a Friday night?* He reached into his pocket and found two cigarettes. He handed them to the pair.

"Yuh ain't got a light, too?"

"You want me to smoke it for you, too?" Donald replied. He found a book of matches in his jacket pocket. "I'm going to have to start charging you," he joked. "Those aren't free, you know."

Fumbling with the book of matches, Ebsary lit one cigarette, handed the other to his companion, Jimmy MacNeil.

"You should have saved some of your booze money for smokes," said Sandy.

"Know where we can get any women?" asked Ebsary. Donald thought the comment seemed strange coming from an older man with greying hair.

"Lots in the park," Donald replied. "None much your age." Yeah, priests, he thought.

"Guess you're right there," said Ebsary. "Want'a come back to the house for a drink?" He gestured to the west, indicating it was not far.

"Maybe another time," Sandy said. "I'm late already."

"'Course, first we would need something to drink," Ebsary said. "Know where we can find a bootlegger, Chief?"

Donald bristled. With one word, the tone changed. *As a Mi'kmaq, he had heard racial taunts all his life. They always stung. When a white man called him chief he knew it was not good.*

"Find your own," Donald replied. "How much did we say we were charging for the cigarettes?" he asked Sandy.

"These guys don't appreciate charity, do they?" Sandy said.

Jimmy MacNeil stumbled while trying to light his cigarette. Donald reached out to steady him.

Ebsary reached into the pocket of his raincoat. "You want money for the cigarette?" he asked, anger in his voice. He began searching his pockets. "We don't much like coloured people and Indians," he added.

MacNeil, weaving on his feet, tried to push Donald away. Though younger, Donald was taller and stronger. He grabbed the guy and held him at arm's length.

"Well, we don't much like drunken bums," Donald said.

Sandy turned to Donald. "What do you think, Junior? Do you like their attitudes?" He stood about a metre from Ebsary, his hands in his pockets. Ebsary groped in his own pocket as though searching for something he couldn't find. "You trying to find your own matches? Maybe you got a pack of cigarettes in there, too. Dig, man, dig."

Ebsary looked at his feet. He fumbled as though looking for loose change. He pulled his hand out, grasping something he tried to hide and lunged at Sandy Seale.

"Here's one for you, Black Boy!"

A flash of a silver blade glinted like a firefly. The old man's hand disappeared in Sandy's midsection. The old man grunted as he lifted the blade and twisted it. Sandy groaned, deeply, and doubled over.

The old guy moved fast, pulling the knife from Sandy's stomach. He turned towards Donald. Donald dropped his grip on the second man.

"There's one for you, too, Indian"

Donald raised his left arm to block the attack. The knife blade caught his arm, two-thirds of the way to his wrist, opening an ugly gash, ten centimetres long.

Stunned for a moment, Donald froze.

2

CHAPTER TWO

DONALD SEEKS HELP

Donald kicked once at Ebsary; he wasn't sure if he had hit him. The old man was faster than he looked, despite being drunk.

Donald jumped back to escape from Ebsary's second swing with the knife.

On the pavement, Sandy sunk down in a heap and lay moaning, holding his gut. Donald knew he was hurt badly.

Donald stepped back once, twice, and then turned to sprint to safety, away from the razor-sharp, slashing blade of the old drunk. Still running, he glanced back to see if he was being pursued.

Twang!

He hit the stop sign with one shoulder. He spun around, twisted once, a full three-sixty, caught his balance again and kept going.

But in looking back he had seen enough.

Sandy had fallen like a sack of potatoes and hadn't moved.

Donald knew his friend needed help. But now, strangely, the street and park seemed deserted.

He sprinted up Byng Avenue, halfway around the block from the park. There, on the deserted midnight streets, he met Maynard Chant.

Maynard was maybe fourteen, from out in the boonies somewhere. He was stocky with a reddish face. Donald had seen him at dances this past year.

He slowed to a walk then stopped.

"Look what they did to me," he said, holding up his left arm, elbow high, so Maynard could see the long cut on his arm.

"Help me," he added. "My buddy is over on the other side of the park with a knife in his stomach."

"Hey, man, you're bleeding!" said Chant.

"S'nothing," Donald replied. "But Sandy's hurt bad. We gotta get help."

They met another group of boys and girls. One girl gave Donald a handkerchief for his wound.

Holding the handkerchief to stem the bleeding, Donald flagged down a passing car, a brown Nova. They repeated the story to the driver.

"Hop in."

Quickly, they were given a lift back to the park to Crescent Street. Sandy still lay where he had fallen. The driver paused long enough for them to get out of the car. He backed up and then drove off.

Sandy was hurt, that much was plain. There was no sign of the two drunks now.

With pleading eyes, Sandy looked up at them. Maynard took off his shirt and held it against the wound in Sandy's midsection. There was blood everywhere, running on the ground, quickly staining Maynard's shirt.

"I'm gonna die," Sandy gasped.

"Stay with him," said Donald.

He sprinted across the street to a grey house and pounded on the door. After what seemed like an hour someone answered.

The resident hesitated and blinked twice. Donald turned to see what the man was now seeing for the first time: one kid hunched over another lying on the street.

Donald quickly told the man what had happened, and showed the cut on his arm. He asked to use the telephone.

"Quick," Donald repeated. "My friend's hurt real bad."

After Donald repeated his story once more, the

resident, Brian Doucette, agreed to call an ambulance. First, though, he called police.

Donald returned to the street and waited with Maynard.

Although they did not know it at the time, when Donald had first met Maynard back on Byng Avenue, one neighbour, a retired RCMP officer, had heard Donald describe the stabbing to Maynard. He, too, had called police. A squad car had been stationed around the corner at the church dance, less than a minute away. As that cruiser arrived on Crescent Street, Donald Marshall Jr. stood in the middle of the road, waving them to the scene and his injured friend.

Minutes later, a second patrol car arrived. Flashing red beacons from the patrol cars now lit up the street: blip, blip, blip.

The first concern of the constables who arrived was to assist Sandy Seale. After confirming that an ambulance was on the way, two officers stayed with Sandy. Noting the cut on Donald's arm, two other constables helped Donald into the second squad car and headed for the hospital.

Shortly after, the ambulance — provided by Leo Curry, ambulance service and funeral director — arrived on the scene. The two police officers helped get Sandy onto a stretcher and into the back of the ambulance, which at other times doubled as a hearse.

Curry exchanged glances with the police officers. One glimpse must have told them all they needed to know: Sandy Seale was gravely injured.

Brian Doucette, the resident Donald had approached, had joined the scene. A hospital orderly, he helped Leo Curry load Sandy into the ambulance and hopped in himself. With a police cruiser flashing its lights leading the way, the ambulance started out on the five-minute drive to St. Rita Hospital.

The few people who had gathered at the scene watched the receding lights, then the reflected glow of the beacon off nearby buildings. The park returned to the stillness of a summer evening in a small waterfront city.

Maynard Chant found himself alone in the dim light of the park. Around him, the crowd disappeared. The sirens weakened in the distance.

He picked up his shirt, now soaked with Sandy Seale's blood, and headed home, thirty-five kilometres away in Louisbourg.

His parents would be angry. Earlier that evening, he had skipped out of church before the last hymn so he could get to the dance.

He headed back to Byng Avenue to resume hitchhiking.

3

CHAPTER THREE

IT LOOKS BAD

At the hospital, experienced doctors and nurses took one look at Sandy's wound and swung into action.

The knife had penetrated through Sandy's midsection and had emerged from his back. The blade had then been lifted and twisted, enlarging the wound. His intestines spilled out of the wound.

The two police officers who had escorted the ambulance on the five-minute drive to the hospital stayed long enough to help undress Sandy.

"I can't breathe," Sandy whispered.

Sandy was moved to a hospital gurney. The ambulance driver helped the surgeon set up an intravenous line into his veins to help replace lost blood with pints of new blood and saline. Sandy had lost a lot of blood.

Police asked to speak to Sandy, but the surgeon refused. The boy's life was at stake.

Within an hour, Sandy's parents, Oscar and Leotha Seale, arrived at the hospital. They had been told only that their son, a charming, church-going teen, had been badly hurt. What could have happened to such a guy, who seldom even missed his midnight curfew?

They were not allowed to see Sandy, and spent the next twenty hours in the agony that is the nightmare of every parent.

★   ★   ★

The incident in Wentworth Park sparked action across Sydney, Nova Scotia.

Because of the wound on his arm, Donald Marshall Jr. had been taken to the hospital by squad car. Staff stitched up the four-inch gash.

At the police station, the duty sergeant called in extra help.

Detective Michael MacDonald had barely made it home from his shift that ended at midnight when he was called in to investigate. He arrived at the hospital in time to help shift Sandy Seale from the ambulance stretcher.

MacDonald spoke briefly to Donald Marshall, who gave him a description of the old guy with the knife:

"One man, heavy set, short, dark blue coat to knees, hair grey, black low shoes, wearing glasses, dark rims. Second man, tall, about five eleven, black hair, clean shaven, corduroy coat three-quarter length, brown in colour."

The description was relayed to all the squad cars in the city.

Both squad cars that responded to the call had arrived at the hospital, stayed long enough to note that hospital staff were in control, and then left to resume normal patrols.

Then, surprisingly, two officers from a third squad car arrived with Maynard Chant in tow.

Maynard hadn't gotten far in his attempt to hitchhike home. He was spotted hitchhiking by officers in another police car — holding his blood-stained shirt.

The two officers had heard the radio chatter and put two and two together. They asked Chant about the stabbing in the park. Chant replied that he "had seen it all." They "invited" him to accompany them to the hospital where he could talk to Detective MacDonald.

Maynard made a shocking sight as he entered the hospital, still carrying his blood-soaked shirt. But Detective MacDonald took it all in stride; he later testified that he viewed Chant as "just a normal hitchhiker."

Despite his claim to have "seen it all," MacDonald took no statement from Chant. Neither did he bother to talk to the first four officers on the scene.

Donald Marshall Jr. had given a good description of the guy with the knife. What more could the detective need?

For a few minutes, Maynard and Donald waited in the hospital corridor.

Donald said, "There were two of them, right?"

Maynard shrugged.

One police officer beckoned to Donald, then led him down the corridor.

"We got two young guys we want you to have a look at," the officer said.

He pointed out two other teens seated in the waiting area.

"Those the guys?" the officer asked.

Donald took one look at the pair and told the officer, "No, that's not them."

On his way out of the hospital, Donald had one last enduring image of Sandy Seale. "The guy had so much blood all over him he shined, his whole body was shiny. I only got a glimpse of him when they were taking his pants off, and I just seen the blood all over him, and I just looked and said to myself, 'Holy man, is that Sandy or what?' But it was him. I knew he was the only one there, the only black guy that was full of blood."

4

CHAPTER FOUR

DONALD AND THE SHIPYARD GANG

After he left the hospital with ten stitches in his arm, Donald Marshall Jr. got special treatment. Two officers gave him a ride home in a squad car.

News of the stabbing travelled fast, even in those long-ago days before text messaging and cell phones. There was no Internet, no Facebook, no Twitter. Phones were reliable but all were land lines with the phone itself bolted to the kitchen wall.

Word travelled nevertheless.

Fast does not always mean accurately, however. The first word to reach the Membertou Reserve, where Donald lived with his parents, shocked those who heard it: Donald Marshall Jr. had been murdered in Wentworth Park.

As the police car drove across the bridge into the reserve, a group of teens had gathered, angered by the news. The group prepared to vent their anger on the Sydney police squad car — until they spotted Donald waving enthusiastically to them through the back window.

Donald was "known to police." In Sydney, N.S., in 1971, that didn't mean quite the same as it might mean in Toronto or Vancouver or Montreal.

Donald had a reputation as a trouble-maker: drinking, hanging out, vandalizing. His family was not poor; that was not the point. His parents worked hard to escape the poverty often affecting natives and other minorities. Both worked: Donald Marshall Sr. as a plasterer and Junior's mother, Caroline, as a cleaner at St. Rita Hospital. As the eldest of the thirteen children — four girls and seven boys and two adopted children — Donald Jr. would inherit his father's title of Grand Chief of the Mi'kmaq in Cape Breton.

But son of the Grand Chief or not, a Native person in Sydney in 1971 was a member of a severely disadvantaged minority and the victim of racism. That racism may have fuelled the anger that Donald carried with him. Though quiet and introspective by nature, a river of anger ran beneath the surface. When the anger ignited, it exploded with violence. He had failed twice by the sixth grade. In the seventh grade and at fifteen years old, he was expelled for striking a teacher. The teacher had tried to grab him by the ear and had pulled a handful of his hair.

Like many who grow up among discrimination and racism, Donald found his refuge with other Mi'kmaq youths in the Shipyard Gang. The gang, lead by Arty Paul, three years older, became an important part of Donald's social life. Gang activity predictably involved drinking, drugs, and vandalism.

But Donald became more than a gang member. Although a loner, an introvert, Donald showed his abilities as a leader. Along with the leader Arty Paul, his gang activities brought him to the attention of police.

In one incident, a bootlegger on the Membertou Reserve was attacked by a group of drunken teens. Late one night, the group ran out of something to drink and woke the bootlegger. The bootlegger refused, and barred his front door with a two-by-four. The teens, including Donald, broke in and took a bottle of wine from the man's fridge.

In the ensuing scuffle, Donald tried to act as peacemaker. For his troubles, the bootlegger hit Donald with a couple of whacks from the two-by-four. Another member of the gang stepped in and the bootlegger received worse. But it was Donald who police charged. In court, he was found not guilty of assault but was sentenced to a day in jail for stealing a bottle of wine.

Girls complicated the picture.

About a year before the stabbing, Donald and his cousin, Tom Christmas, dated the same girl. One night, the girl's mother barged in on the trio. Tom escaped out the back door, but Donald was still struggling to get dressed. When the case came to court on a charge of rape, the girl admitted to having an affair with the two for six months. The case was dismissed.

During that same year before the stabbing — when Donald and his friends were sixteen and seventeen years of age — police increasingly would round up gang members as though on a hunch. This may have been because officers targeted the native kids, but many in the gang thought one of their members was acting as a police snitch.

High on the list of suspected informants was the only non-Mi'kmaq in the gang: John Pratico. A thin, wispy guy with thick, black, unruly hair, John was a troubled sixteen-year-old, and a heavy drinker. He was under the care of a psychiatrist who later described him as someone with "a rather childish desire to be in the limelight or centre of attention."

The Shipyard Gang saw Pratico as a weakling, someone in need of support.

★   ★   ★

After his taxi ride home in the squad car, Donald re-
told his story of the events that night. Some time after 2
a.m., he met his cousins Tom and Kevin Christmas. He
repeated the story.

Alone with his cousins, Donald started to face the
reality of the situation. What if Sandy was not alright?
He didn't look that good when he last saw him in the
hospital.

Kevin was rather blunt, suggesting that Donald would
be a police suspect in the stabbing.

Alarmed, and desperate, Donald and cousin Tom
rode on bicycles back to Wentworth Park. Wordlessly,
they rode around, not wanting to disturb neighbours and
bring in the police yet again.

They found nothing: no knife, no assailants, only the
cool deserted night air drifting over the ponds from the
harbour.

Donald began to worry.

5

CHAPTER FIVE

MACINTYRE IN ACTION

The next morning, a Saturday, Sergeant of Detectives, John MacIntyre, swept into the police station.

A big man, 260 pounds, he was not the type who could slip by anyone unnoticed.

At his desk, he grabbed a fistful of reports from the night before.

"The stabbing in here?" he asked no one in particular.

He flipped through the reports. Drunks. Fender benders. Nothing worthy of the time of a detective. Except the stabbing.

The evening before, he had not felt well and had gone to bed early. At 3 a.m. he got a call from the desk sergeant telling him of the stabbing. *Christ*, he thought. *By then the stabbing was three hours old. What did they expect him to do?*

In the office, Detective MacDonald lingered nearby.

"So somebody got a black kid last night?" MacIntyre asked him.

MacDonald shrugged. "Not one of our usual clients," he answered. "But the guy he was with, you'll recognize his name."

"Indian?" asked MacIntyre.

"Donald Marshall."

MacIntyre shifted his weight in his groaning chair. "Why did I suspect that?" he said. The big officer and Donald Marshall Jr. had a history.

A few months before, the Shipyard Gang had taken a drinking party to a cemetery. This led to a rampage of tombstones. Damages totalled $19,000. The main target of the vandalism was a huge headstone for a family named MacIntyre. It was knocked down, apparently, because MacIntyre, the cop, was loathed by the young natives.

Right away — perhaps tipped off by an informant within the gang — MacIntyre pulled Donald in for an interview. Donald admitted being in the cemetery but denied doing the damage. He knew who did, he told the detective, but finding out was the job of the police.

So when Donald Marshall Jr.'s name was linked to the stabbing at Wentworth Park, MacIntyre was not surprised. He leaned back in his chair, his arms behind his head.

"Okay," he said to Detective MacDonald, "tell me what you got."

Maybe, he thought, *this would be the big one he'd pin on Marshall.*

MacDonald flipped through his notes. "Marshall says it was some old guy dressed like a priest, who whipped out a knife and got the kid. We broadcast his description. I told the patrols to keep looking around — maybe somebody would come back into the park fitting the description — and if they wanted to look around the park area, you know, if they had a few minutes to spare from their regular patrol."

"What shape's the black kid in?"

"Not good. He lost a lot of blood. Internal damage. He was almost gutted."

MacIntyre drummed his fingers on the desk.

"Anything from the scene?"

"After I was finished at the hospital I drove down to the Crescent Street area and drove through the park."

"Find anything?"

"I got out of my car and took my flashlight and walked around the sidewalk by the houses, looking to see if I might pick up something."

"This was where, what's his name," — MacIntyre looked down his glasses at the report in his hand — "Seale, was found?"

"Not exactly."

"What did you find?"

MacDonald spread his hands open in front of him: "Nothing."

MacIntyre breathed out of flared nostrils. He gave MacDonald a dismissive wave with the back of his hand. "This is your day off, right?" he said. "Take off. I got it from here."

After flipping through the rest of the crime reports from the night before, MacIntyre drove to the park. *You never know*, he thought. *It would have been nice if the area had been secured, but that would have meant pulling someone off patrol.*

Still, he better have a look now, even if the scene was ten hours old.

With one uniformed officer, MacIntyre visited the park. The constable found one bloodied tissue. Nothing else.

Wentworth Park looked, smelled, acted differently in the middle of an early June Saturday morning. The teens from the dance were long gone. People who lived in the houses along Crescent Street across from the park had gone about their business. *Most had likely slept through the ruckus the night before*, he thought.

On the way back to the station, MacIntyre stopped to chat with Sergeant Murray Wood of the RCMP.

He outlined the events from the night before, as he understood them.

"Got any leads?" asked the Mountie.

MacIntyre hesitated. "I don't think I have to look very far," he said. "You know who the second guy was?"

Wood said he did not.

"Donald Marshall."

The Mountie crossed his arms as though denying this hunch. *MacIntyre seemed always ready to blame everything on Indians.* Wood had his doubts. "There was an incident in Rotary Park a couple of weeks ago, something about a guy with a knife," he said. "Anything come of that?"

"No connection," MacIntyre snapped. "Anyway, I've a pretty good idea who did this."

The Mountie lifted an eyebrow, waiting for MacIntyre to finish his thought.

"Know what I think?" MacIntyre added, as though on cue. "I think Marshall's description of some old guy is a crock. The whole thing likely happened when that Indian, fueled up with fire water, got in an argument with the black kid."

"Any proof?"

"I'll get proof," MacIntyre replied.

As head of the detectives in Sydney, MacIntyre had plenty of face time with Marshall. The Shipyard Gang had given him plenty of trouble. *Well,* he thought, *maybe this would end it.*

So by noon on Saturday, the stabbing was less than twelve hours hold. There was no evidence but a facial tissue soaked in blood and a black youth in surgery. Still, MacIntyre had already formed a theory about who did it: Donald Marshall Jr.

Standard police procedures at the time required that the scene of the stabbing be secured — roped off with the yellow police tape with officers standing guard. Detective "Red Mike" MacDonald, the first detective on the case, didn't bother with taking statements. He talked only briefly to Donald Marshall, dismissed Maynard Chant, apparently didn't ask Sandy Seale about what happened (on arrival at the hospital, barely conscious), and made no effort to direct officers who did respond to the scene in gathering evidence. The oversight was later described as the ultimate in police incompetence.

On Saturday, Sandy Seale lay near death in the same hospital that employed Donald's mother as a cleaner. MacIntyre made no effort, either, to find and talk to any of the people who had been in the park that fatal Friday night.

But MacIntyre didn't need to waste time on detailed investigations; he thought he knew who did it.

A few months before the stabbing, MacIntyre told
Emily Clemens, the mother of Donald's girlfriend at the
time, that Donald "would make the mistake sometime
in the near future that he would probably ... get him —
pick him up on it."

Well, maybe this was the time. All he had to do was
prove it. And he had a pipeline into the Shipyard Gang
that might help him do just that.

⁂

But if MacIntyre did little that Saturday in the way of
real investigation, Donald Marshall was not so complacent. His cousin had said that if the police could not
find the guy with the knife, they would blame him. That
comment had struck home.

He knew the investigation would be handled by
MacIntyre. And he had enough experience with the big
police officer that he didn't expect kid gloves.

Rather than wait, Donald and another cousin set
out on Saturday afternoon to find the old man with the
knife. The old guy had invited Sandy and him back to
his house, Donald recalled, and had indicated it was a
residence within a block or two.

But before they could start their door-to-door calling,

police arrived and hustled Donald back to the station. The investigating, they said, would be done by police.

Uncharacteristically, Donald obeyed. At MacIntyre's request, he stuck around the police station all day in case they needed more information.

At the hospital, Sandy's frantic parents waited. Sandy underwent two emergency surgeries in an attempt to save his life.

The attempts failed.

Shortly before 8 p.m. on May 29, Sandy Seale, seventeen years old, an elite hockey player, an athletic, church-going black youth in Sydney, Nova Scotia, died of his wounds.

The incident in Wentworth Park now changed from an inept major crime investigation to an inept murder investigation.

6

CHAPTER SIX

DONALD TELLS HIS STORY

The news of Sandy's death hit Donald hard.

Although they were not close friends, they shared interests. Just less than twenty-four hours earlier, they had been two young guys cruising a park looking for some excitement: girls, drinks, whatever.

Now, one of them was dead. When you are seventeen, death is for old people.

Donald had spent most of the day Saturday hanging around the police station. When he heard of Sandy's death, he returned home. Normally, he would avoid the police station at any time; he did not view police as his friends.

But this was different. Frightened, confused, not even sure of his own memories of the event, he realized that he both feared the police and relied on them.

On Sunday, he returned to the police station. Police

had assembled a lineup. They wanted Donald to see if he could identify the killer from the group.

All but one of the guys in the lineup had been young. The older guy definitely was not the one who stabbed Sandy. About mid-morning, Donald left the police station to walk the four kilometres home.

On Bentinck Street, he met John Pratico and a couple of other guys sitting on Pratico's porch. He took the cigarette that was offered to him and again repeated the story of the events surrounding the stabbing.

Pratico, the only non-native member of the Shipyard Gang, listened with keen attention. He even volunteered to help Donald look for the old guy who Donald still thought lived in the neighbourhood. Donald thanked him for the offer. Pratico owed him. The week before, Donald had rescued him from three toughs who thought he made a good punching bag.

Later on Sunday afternoon, Donald was summoned once again to the police station by MacIntyre. Even though he had spent considerable time with police after the stabbing, no one had taken a formal statement from him.

When he arrived at the station, Donald found himself on the hard benches outside the detective's office with Maynard Chant and John Pratico. Maynard being there was no surprise. He was the first person he had talked to after Sandy got stabbed, and he had helped out. But Pratico? Donald couldn't recall seeing him that night.

"Marshall!" Sergeant of Detectives MacIntyre bellowed from the doorway of the detective's office.

Donald shuffled in, leaving Chant and Pratico behind. MacIntyre motioned to a chair.

"Tell us what happened, Marshall."

"I told it a dozen times."

"Well, tell it one more time. This time we want to make it … official." Donald held the big man's gaze. He could hear the contempt in the officer's voice. Many times he had sat across from the huge officer. He had never tried to hide his anger and contempt.

But this time was different. This time, his anger was turned outward, at the old guy with white hair and dark raincoat who had stabbed his friend. This time he needed, even trusted, the police to find the guy. He had spent hours that day, and the day before, at the police station, ready to be of help.

"This time we'll put it on record," MacIntyre added. "We'll need you to sign the statement."

Donald nodded.

Donald told of meeting Bobby Patterson, the young guy who had been vomiting in the park. Assured that

Patterson at least knew them by name — a sobriety test of sorts — he said he and Sandy continued through the park towards the bridge.

"We stood there for a few seconds," he said. "Two men whom we did not know called us up from Crescent Street. They asked us for two cigarettes. I gave them to them. Also a book of matches."

"And then?"

"The old guy started to talk to me about women. I said, 'Lots of them in the park'; also they wanted to know where a bootlegger was."

Donald didn't bother to mention that both of them were drunk.

"Who were these guys?" asked MacIntyre.

"I asked them where they were from and they said Manitoba. I asked them if you guys were priests and the tall fellow said, 'We are.' One fellow had a long, blue coat on. They told us 'we don't like coloured people or Indians.'"

"I bet that made you angry," said the detective.

Donald continued: "The old guy turned to Sandy and said, 'There is one for you, black boy, and he put the knife in his stomach. Then he took the knife out of Sandy and swung at me and put it in my left arm. He told me, 'There is one for you, too, Indian.'

Donald held up his arm to show the bandages.

"And what did you do then?"

"I stood there for two seconds and then ran for help."

MacIntyre stood, with one leg up on a chair, resting his elbow on his knee. He took a drag on his cigarette and blew the smoke in Donald's direction.

"Did you know these fellows?" he asked.

"No."

"Did you ever see them before?"

"No."

"Describe them."

Donald repeated his description: "One fellow, the small fellow, was five foot nine, one-hundred-ninety pounds, hair grey, combed back. Wore black rimmed glasses, age fifty years. He had a long wide face, and wore a long, blue coat, a dark sweater. He had black shoes with rounded toes."

"Good. And the other guy?"

"The other fellow, brown corduroy short coat, five foot eleven inches, about one-hundred-fifty pounds, hair black, short hair. Age thirty-five years. He was wearing a blue sweater, too, with a V-neck with buttons. Both of them had thin faces."

MacIntyre stubbed out his cigarette. The air in the room was blue. He waved his hands over the ashtray in an attempt to clear the air.

"Anything you'd like to add?"

Donald shrugged. He didn't like talking to cops. Especially this cop. He always told them little. But this was different. Sandy was dead.

"Are you going to catch these guys?" Donald asked.

"We'll get the guy who stabbed Sandy," MacIntyre replied, his eyes fixed on Donald. "You can be sure of that."

Donald looked away first.

"We've written down just what you told us. You'll have to sign it now as an official statement."

Donald shook his head.

"It becomes part of the record," MacIntyre stressed. "If you're lying, it will come out."

"Ain't lyin'."

MacIntyre locked eyes with the youth.

"Okay then."

He held the door open for Marshall.

The entire interview had lasted twenty-two minutes.

7

CHAPTER SEVEN

MAYNARD INVENTS

MacIntyre blocked the doorway into the detective office as Donald Marshall returned to his seat on the hard benches in the hall.

"Marshall, you wait on the bench over there and we'll have that statement ready for you to sign."

MacIntyre had set up the interviews this way on purpose. He wanted Marshall to know that he had his story on record. *With any luck, the next two would contradict Marshall, and he would be able to pry open the truth.*

His years of experience told him that Marshall was not telling the truth. *Usually cheeky and mouthy, Marshall appeared more subdued than he had ever seen him. Not that this was proof, but when people start lying, they don't know how to act. So they change.*

He pointed at Maynard Chant.

"You're next, Chant."

Chant, fourteen years old and in the seventh grade, rose from the bench. Marshall and Chant exchanged glances in passing. Detective MacIntyre was pleased. *He wanted these two to know that their stories had better match.*

Maynard squeezed past the big officer in the doorway and took his seat. Sgt. MacIntyre closed the door behind him.

"Tell us what happened, Maynard."

To Maynard, this should have been easy: he saw nothing of the events until Donald found him on Byng Avenue and they returned to the site of the stabbing.

"I didn't see anything," he told police.

"We have a witness who said you were there."

"Where?"

"In the park. That you saw it all."

Police did have a witness. When Maynard started hitch-hiking home that night, he got a short ride in a pickup truck. The driver of the truck later contacted police, thinking that Maynard was the key to the events of the evening. Perhaps Maynard had told the man, as he did the two police officers who picked him up, that he "had seen it all." What he had likely meant was that he had returned with Donald to help Sandy. But for Sgt. MacIntyre, Maynard was the key he needed to unlock this.

"We have a witness who puts you in the park," MacIntyre said.

"I wasn't."

MacIntyre let impatience show in his voice. "Maynard, you know how this works. You tell us the truth, and we go easy. Lie to us, and you'll go to jail."

"Jail?"

"You're already on probation over that caper with the milk bottles," said MacIntyre. "You admit drinking. That's a violation of probation right there. And against the law in the first place, at your age."

"Well, I …"

"We wouldn't have to look very far even without this stabbing to find enough to put you away," said Sgt. MacIntyre. "So right now we need the truth."

Maynard shifted in his seat. *If the truth of what he had or had not seen did not work, then he would tell what he knew. And all he knew of the stabbing is what Donald had told him.*

If that's the story they wanted, he would give it.

"Okay, then," said Maynard. "I was walking across the railway tracks in Wentworth Park."

"And?"

"I seen two fellows walking and two more walking kind of slow, talking. The two fellows who stabbed Donald Marshall and Sandy Seale: they talked for a few minutes over on Crescent Street."

"Get to the point."

"One fellow hauled a knife from his pocket and stabbed one of the fellows. So I took off back across the tracks to Byng Avenue and started to walk towards the bus terminal.

"Then I see Donald Marshall coming down. I turned around and started to walk the other way. Donald caught up with me and said, 'Look what they did to me.' He showed me a long cut on his left arm. Then he said, 'Help me, my buddy is over on the other side of the park with a knife in his stomach.' Then we started to look for more help."

"Did you see anyone else?"

"He met some boys and girls. One of the girls gave Donald a handkerchief. We got in a car to take us over to where Seale was lying on the pavement."

"That's when you tried to help Sandy?" asked the officer.

"I took my shirt and put it around his waist, and Donald went to a grey house and asked the man if he would call an ambulance."

"That's it?"

"Well, after the police and ambulance arrived, I figured I better get home. So I left."

"And that's when the officers picked you up?"

"Yeah. Took me to the hospital. Called my dad."

"But nothing more about the stabbing?"

"Nope."

MacIntyre appeared to relax. "Good work, Maynard. Now can you describe the two men? It would help us a lot to find them."

Maynard struggled, but provided a few details: "One man, about six foot two, light brown hair, dark pants, suit coat, over two hundred pounds. The other fellow six-feet tall, dark pants, dark hair, one-hundred-sixty-five pounds."

It was a wildly inaccurate description, but the best he could remember from what Donald had told him.

At the time, Maynard thought it was a helpful lie.

MacIntyre repeated his spiel about typing up the statement to be signed, and Maynard was sent into the hallway to wait.

"Pratico, you're next."

8

CHAPTER EIGHT

PRATICO FABRICATES

MacIntyre had "invited" John Pratico to give a statement based only on a hunch. The guy MacIntyre had
hired to paint his house lived close to the Pratico
family.

Earlier that day, the painter had overheard Marshall
telling Pratico and his friends about the stabbing. The
painter had thought Pratico had been in the park and
would be worth talking to.

Aside from his theory that Marshall stabbed Sandy,
MacIntyre had little to go on. He was willing to squeeze
anybody to break Marshall's story. And Pratico had
always proven to be a good source on the activities of
the Shipyard Gang.

Now, MacIntyre was prepared to add some
pressure.

All that John Pratico knew about the stabbing was

what Donald had told him that morning. That didn't stop him, either, from creating a story of his own.

What MacIntyre didn't know — and didn't want to hear — was the truth: John Pratico had gone to the dance at St. Joseph's Church hall. He had drunk far, far too much. Several Mi'kmaq friends from the Shipyard Gang had taken him to a nearby lumberyard to sober up and to keep him out of the eyes of police.

But MacIntyre had a different agenda now. He leaned forward in his chair, his massive elbows splayed across the desk.

"Tell us where you were Friday night. Where did you go? What did you do?"

MacIntyre could smell fear. Pratico was a mousy, timid kid. He'd talk.

"I went to the dance."

"At the church hall?"

"Yes."

"What time did you leave?"

John pondered, only for a moment.

"About midnight."

"Did you meet anyone?"

"Yeah, Donald Marshall. And Sandy Seale."

"Did you stay with them long?"

Pratico said he met the two only briefly. "Then I went

down Argyle Street and over to Crescent Street." He said he continued on to the courthouse, farther down on the extension of Crescent.

MacIntyre pried for details. "What exactly did you see?"

"I was over by the courthouse when I heard a scream."

"And then?"

"I saw two men running away from the stabbing scene."

"What did they do?"

"They jumped into a white Volkswagen."

"Did you know these two?"

"No, but Bobby Patterson told me they were from a Toronto bike gang."

MacIntyre pried for more details, but every time he started to add to his story, Pratico contradicted himself.

Pratico's description of the two men was markedly different from the description given by either Chant or Marshall.

MacIntyre had a problem. He had statements from three people with differing versions of a story. He had a suspect who admitted to being at the scene: Donald Marshall Jr.

He knew that at least one, maybe two, perhaps all three were lying in some part of their stories.

But he needed someone, a witness, or maybe two, who had been at the scene and had really seen what had happened.

If he couldn't find such a witness, he would create one instead.

CHAPTER NINE

PRATICO'S SECOND STORY

JUNE 4TH: THE MORNING

MacIntyre knew that the signed statements from Donald Marshall, Maynard Chant and John Pratico were a good start.

The statements didn't jibe with his policeman's hunch — which would later prove to be wrong — that told him that Donald Marshall Jr. stabbed Sandy. To prove this, he needed at least one witness who could blow holes in Marshall's story.

John Pratico's statement didn't quite fit. *There was something about it that the senior police officer could not quite believe.* This proved to be a valid hunch, since Pratico lied from the outset. But it drove MacIntyre in the wrong direction, based on his racist attitudes.

A day or two after he had taken the statements from the three teens, MacIntyre made another trip to

Wentworth Park. *This time he was going to play detective. He had gone over Pratico's statement, and needed to assure himself that Pratico could actually see what he said he could see.*

He tried tracing the events on a map of the park and encountered a problem: Pratico couldn't see anything from the courthouse, where he had heard screams. Nor from that distance could he have seen people jumping into a white Volkswagen. *If, indeed, there had been a white Volkswagen.*

On the morning of Friday, June 4, almost one week after the murder, MacIntyre picked up Pratico again for another talk. This time, the gloves came off.

First they went for a stroll — literally, a walk in the park. Wentworth Park.

There, MacIntyre turned to Pratico. First, they stood near the spot where the stabbing took place.

"This time I want you to tell me the truth," MacIntyre said.

"I told you the truth," Pratico replied.

MacIntyre towered over him. "Look, I want to make this easy on you," he said. "We have a witness saying you were in the park that night. Right near this spot."

"I wasn't."

"Okay, let's start at the beginning," said the big officer.

"You said you were at the courthouse when you heard the screams."

"Yeah, over that way." Pratico pointed down the street. The courthouse was half a block away, and around a bend.

"That's a couple of hundred yards from here," MacIntyre said. "You could maybe have heard screams from there but could not have seen anything."

"But I did; the two guys came running and jumped into a white …"

"Yeah, white Volkswagen. The great mystery car. It's like a magical white rabbit, John. There was no such car. And if there was, you couldn't see it from the courthouse."

Pratico stared at the ground, stunned.

"Now," said MacIntyre, "I want you to tell the truth. We have someone who saw you in the park."

"I wasn't."

"You are lying."

"I'm telling the truth!"

MacIntyre's voice rose. "Do you want to end up in jail?"

"Jail?"

"It's called perjury," yelled the detective. "If you don't tell me the truth, it's perjury. You can go to jail for perjury." The detective rose to his full height. He spat out the words: "Now. Tell. Me. The. Truth."

"But I …"

MacIntyre started rummaging through his keys as though looking for the right one to lock up his young witness.

"Tell me the truth, and you won't end up in jail."

John Pratico trembled. Jail was a real threat to him.

"Our witness has you somewhere near where we are standing," said MacIntyre.

Pratico swallowed hard. The lump in his throat hurt. He nodded.

"Want to show me where? Behind that bush?" asked the officer.

Pratico nodded. "Yeah, that one," he said, pointing to the same shrub the detective had indicated.

"Trying to hide while drinking beer, eh?" said MacIntyre.

"Yeah, I guess." Pratico, now deep in the lie, needed to follow the policeman's lead.

"Did you see Donald Marshall stab Sandy Seale?"

John Pratico nodded.

"Good. Now we're getting somewhere. Let's go down to the station now, and we can get this all down on paper. And then this will be over, John."

Always willing to help, especially when people yelled

at him, John Pratico wiped away tears and nodded.

Then politely, he got back in the police car with MacIntyre. Back at the police station the detective was much more friendly. In the detective's office, they gave Pratico a soft drink and even offered him a cigarette.

The big officer almost smiled. "All set, John? Let's start at the beginning. You don't have to protect Donald Marshall. Where were you last Friday night?"

"Last Friday night I went to the dance at St. Joseph's hall, George Street, Sydney ..."

"Last Friday? That's a week ago today?"

Pratico nodded.

"I went with Bobby Christmas. Donald Gordon and I met Bob James from Alexander Street there. He gave me money to get in."

"What time was this?"

"About nine-thirty p.m. I was at the dance until about ten or five to twelve. Then I went out by myself."

"Did you meet Donald Marshall and Sandy Seale?"

"Yeah. We walked to the corner of Argyle Street. Donald said, 'John, come down to the park.' In a rough voice. I said, 'No.'"

"Where did you go then?"

"I went down Argyle Street and over to Crescent Street. I was walking on the park side. I seen Sandy and

Donald on the other side of the bridge, stopped. I did not pay much attention to them."

"But where did you go?"

"I kept walking on the tracks. I stopped where I showed you."

The police detective nodded. "You were behind the shrub near the tracks?"

"Yes."

"So Sandy and Donald were standing about where the incident happened?"

"Right."

"Did you hear them arguing?"

"I heard Sandy say to Junior, 'You crazy Indian' and then Junior called him a black bastard."

"What else did they say?"

"They were still arguing. They were talking low. I could not make out what they were saying."

MacIntyre leaned closer to Pratico and lowered his voice.

"Which way was Sandy Seale facing?

"Facing the tracks."

"Was Donald Marshall facing the street?"

"Yeah."

"How close were they?"

"Arm's length."

"What did you see or hear next?"

"I did not hear. I …"

"Did you see Donald Marshall stab Sandy Seale?"

"I just seen Donald Marshall's hand going towards the left side of Seale's stomach. He drove his hand in — turned it and pulled it back."

"What happened then?" asked the officer.

John blinked. He was not sure.

"That's when Sandy fell to the ground?"

"Yeah."

"And Donald Marshall ran up Crescent Street towards Argyle."

"Yeah, that's what happened."

Detective MacIntyre smiled at Pratico. "You're doing fine, John. Just fine. So then what did you do?"

"I …"

"Relax, John. Just tell us the truth. Tell us what you did next."

"I run home up Bentinck Street."

"Were you standing on the tracks at the time Sandy Seale fell to the ground?"

"Yes, I was."

"Why were you standing there?"

"I was drinking a bottle of beer."

Detective MacIntyre smirked. "We'll have your

statement typed up. You'll have to sign it," he told the hollow-eyed youth. "Then you're free to go home."

"No jail?"

The detective patted John Pratico on the shoulder.

"No jail, John. You've been a very good boy."

10

CHAPTER TEN

ANOTHER STORY CHANGES

JUNE 4TH: THE AFTERNOON

When the Louisbourg police arrived at his door that same afternoon, June 4, Maynard Chant felt familiar chills of fear. Police knocking on his door was nothing new. And it never ended well.

"Some officers from Sydney want to talk to him," the officer standing at the door told his mother.

Cautiously, Maynard came to the door. The officer was Louisbourg Police Chief Wayne Magee. In a small town like Louisbourg, everyone knew him.

"We have to go all the way to Sydney?" Maynard asked, accepting the inevitable. *He assumed that when police asked, you had to talk to them.*

And there was that thing about money in the milk bottles. He had been caught stealing. He was still on probation.

"Nope," replied the chief. "Just down at the town

hall." He indicated the squad car. "Got your taxi waiting."

The room used for the interview was a bit crowded. In addition to Chant and his mother, Chant's probation officer, Lawrence Burke, was in the room. And, of course, Detectives MacIntyre and William Urquhart and Louisbourg Police Chief Wayne Magee.

MacIntyre lost little time in niceties about the weather.

"We need you to go over your statement one more time," he said. "We're trying to fill in the gaps."

Maynard nodded.

"Just tell the truth, son," said his mother beside him. "That's all the officers want."

"That's true, Ma'am," said MacIntyre. "But I prefer if you let the boy answer."

There was silence for a moment.

"Okay, Maynard," said the detective, a big man with a loose tie. "You told us earlier this week that you had seen a man stab Sandy Seale, and that you then turned along the railway tracks to Byng Avenue."

Maynard nodded. "That's right."

"And then Marshall caught up with you."

"Yeah."

"Okay, I need you to describe the man who stabbed Sandy."

"Well, I ..."

"Tall, short, old, young, how was he dressed?"

"I don't know."

"You don't know?"

Even though he had fabricated a description five days earlier, Maynard grabbed the quickest answer:

"It was dark."

"Yet you could identify Donald Marshall and Sandy Seale, right?"

"Well, I knew them. I never saw the two men before."

MacIntyre rose from his chair and leaned towards the boy, with his knuckles on the table.

The officer talked slowly, his deep voice rattling windows: "You can't describe them because you didn't see them, is that right?"

Maynard said nothing.

"I'm saying right now that I think Donald Marshall told you that there were two men," he said. "But you did not see them."

Maynard nodded. At the police station on Sunday night, the day after Sandy had died, Donald Marshall had been angry, upset. While they had waited in the hallway outside the detective's office, Donald kept saying, "There were two of them, weren't there?" So, now, to give the police what they wanted, Maynard said he had seen them, too.

He had lied.

The officer leaned across the table, his face less than a foot away.

"Now tell us the truth, damn it! There were no two men, right?"

Maynard glanced up at the big man and then looked away. He said nothing.

"Look, we know you're lying, and that can revoke your probation and get you two to five years in jail. Did you know that?"

Maynard shook his head.

"So the truth. There were no two men."

Maynard looked at his mother and shrugged. What's the use, he thought.

"That's right."

The officer stood up and fiddled with the pen on the table by his notebook. "Good, that's a start."

"Now what did you see?"

Maynard shrugged.

"Okay, let's start from the beginning." MacIntyre pulled a piece of paper out of the notebook and glanced at it.

"You left the dance about eleven-thirty p.m. What did you do then?"

"I walked down the tracks towards George Street."

"Okay, now answer this carefully: tell us who you saw."

Maynard gave another sullen shrug.

"Maynard, you're on probation, right?"

Maynard nodded.

"Of course you are. That's why Mr. Burke, your probation officer is here. Now, I don't want to see you go to jail over this thing, because you had just tried to help, right?"

Maynard nodded.

"Okay, now answer this carefully. We have another witness who saw you in the park that night. So tell us the truth because we know when you are lying." *There was no "other witness," but the lie had worked on John Pratico that morning. It was worth trying again.*

Maynard looked at his mother. She leaned forward, placed a hand on his arm.

"Just tell them the truth," she repeated.

MacIntyre turned his attention to Mrs. Chant. "Mrs. Chant, you are here as an observer as a courtesy. If you interfere, I'm going to have to ask you to leave the room." He turned back to Maynard. "Now, let's get to the first point. You say you were on the tracks. Can you see the bridge from there?"

"I don't …"

"And the bandshell. Can you see that from where you were standing?"

"Hmmm."

"See, Maynard, that's the problem we have with what you told us Sunday. You could not see from where you were. Did you see a dark-haired fellow sort of hiding in the bushes?"

"I ..."

"Don't you put words in his mouth!" said Mrs. Chant. "Let him tell what he saw!"

Detective MacIntyre straightened up. He looked resigned.

"Mrs. Chant, I'm going to have to ask you to leave the room. Chief Magee, will you escort Mrs. Chant out, make sure she is comfortable? We may be a while."

Gently but firmly, Police Chief Magee guided Mrs. Chant by the elbow and steered her from the room. Maynard watched his mother leave. When the door closed, he turned back to the detective.

Detective MacIntyre locked eyes with Maynard. "This dark-haired fellow. Did you know him?"

"Who?"

"This dark-haired fellow. Hiding behind that bush by the tracks. Did you know him?"

"Not by name. But I seen him at dances in

Louisbourg," said Maynard.

"Okay, now we're getting somewhere. Did you see him since?"

"Sunday afternoon at the police office in Sydney."

"That would be John Pratico."

Maynard nodded.

MacIntyre looked almost friendly now. "That was while you were waiting to give me your earlier statement," he said.

"Yeah."

"Okay, back to that night. You're on the railway tracks. You look out to Crescent Street."

"Yeah. First, I walked by this guy on the tracks. I looked back to see what he was looking at."

"And that's when you see two guys on Crescent Street."

"They were standing about one-and-a-half feet from each other."

"Were they the same size?"

"One was smaller than the other."

"Which one was facing you?"

"Short, dark fellow was facing the tracks. The taller man was facing the houses."

"Did you recognize either of these men?"

"The only man I recognized was Donald Marshall."

"What was he wearing?"

"Dark pants. I think a yellow shirt with sleeves up to the elbows."

"Up to his elbows?" MacIntyre glowered. Maynard flinched. "And they were arguing?" the officer added.

"Yeah. When he was arguing, I mean Donald Marshall with the other man, his sleeves were down to his wrist. At that time."

"How long were you on the tracks watching them?"

"About five minutes."

"Could you hear what they were talking about?"

"No, I just heard a mumbling of swearing. I think Marshall was the one who was doing most of the swearing."

"Is that when Marshall pulled out his knife?"

Maynard hesitated and exchanged glances with his probation officer. "I seen Marshall haul a knife from his pocket and jab the other fellow with it in the side of the stomach."

MacIntyre blew a sigh of relief. *He had what he needed.* He had Chant sign every page of the handwritten statement. *With two witnesses who claimed to have seen Marshall stab Sandy Seale, the case was almost locked up.* Shortly after the interview ended, Detectives MacIntyre and Urquhart left for Sydney.

It was time to arrest Donald Marshall Jr. for the murder of Sandy Seale.

11

CHAPTER ELEVEN

DONALD IS ARRESTED

JUNE 4TH: THE EVENING

Donald Marshall was changing a light bulb in his grand-parents' house when an unmarked RCMP car pulled into the driveway.

The fluorescent bulb flickered in his hands. He climbed down from the chair. The bulb gave one last flicker and died.

At the doorway, his father blocked his way.

"What's going on?" Donald asked.

Donald was tense, his anger not far from the surface. During the past few days he had received death threats, anonymous callers who called him a killer. To escape the threats, the family had driven to nearby Whycocomagh, 115 kilometres from Membertou and Sydney.

Community reaction to the death of Sandy Seale had been strong. Many in the black community thought

Donald was the killer. Tensions were building.

Donald did not attend Sandy's funeral for that reason. Before the funeral, he had visited the funeral home twice. The first time he had shaken hands with Sandy's oldest brother and told him how sorry he was. On a second visit he did not know how to act. He was Roman Catholic; he thought that Sandy was Protestant. He didn't want to bless him, or pray, because he didn't know what Protestants did. He stood silently by the casket for several minutes, locked in his own thoughts and inward prayers.

While he was in the funeral home, a fight had broken out in the parking lot between blacks and some of the Shipyard Gang who had accompanied Donald.

In spite of the wild ways he had adopted — not abnormal for the time and place — Donald at seventeen was still very much a boy. Earlier that day, he had tried to help a group of five-year-old kids at Membertou catch ducks. The ducks won, and Donald ended up soaked to the skin.

Now, he faced his father in the doorway to his grand-father's house, one month after the death of his grand-father and one week after the stabbing of Sandy Seale. All of a sudden he was grown up.

His father asked if he had killed Sandy Seale.

"No," Donald replied.

His father held him by the shoulders and looked him in the eye. The look said he had no choice. "And don't give them any trouble," his father added, knowing that Donald's anger could be his worst enemy.

His mother sobbed uncontrollably.

Donald kissed her and allowed himself to be led away.

12

CHAPTER TWELVE

ANOTHER WITNESS INVENTION

With Donald Marshall Jr. in jail, MacIntyre now wanted information only if it supported the case against Marshall. No efforts were made to find the mysterious two men — the two drunks — who Marshall said had been involved.

Donald Marshall had told police from the beginning that he had talked to Patricia Harriss and Terry Gushue just prior to the stabbing. Yet it was a full two weeks before MacIntyre got around to checking that out.

Finally, on June 17 — twenty days after the stabbing and a day less than two weeks after Donald Marshall was arrested — MacIntyre did talk to Patricia Harriss.

A police car picked her up at home with her mother about 7:30 p.m. that evening. Patricia was only fourteen; she was in the seventh grade. It was not only normal but expected that a parent would be present. At the station they were met by Detective William Urquhart.

Somewhat confused as to why she was being summoned now to tell her story, Patricia tried to provide as much information as she could to the officers.

The night of the stabbing, she said, she had gone to the dance at St. Joseph's Church hall. About 11:45 p.m., she left with her boyfriend, Terry Gushue.

"We sat on a bench near the bandstand," she said. "Robert Patterson was on the grass sick, throwing up. We smoked a cigarette."

Detective Urquhart prompted her. "And then?"

"Terry and I left. We walked back behind the bandshell onto Crescent Street in front of the big green building. We saw and talked to Junior Marshall."

"Who else was there?" asked Urquhart.

"With Marshall was two other men."

"Describe the other men to me," said the officer.

"One man was short with a long coat. Grey or white hair, with a long coat. I was talking to Junior. Terry got a match from Junior, and Junior said they were crazy. They were asking him, Junior, for a cigarette."

"Did you see Sandy Seale in the park?"

"No."

"Was there anyone else in the park?"

"Yes, boys and girls walking through the park. Gussie Dobbin and Kenny Barrow, they left while we were still on the bench."

Detective Urquhart had been taking notes. Detective MacIntyre came into the room. He motioned to Urquhart, and both men left the room.

Patricia and her mother waited for some time. Eventually, the two officers returned. This time MacIntyre took over the questioning. He was a big man and he frightened Patricia.

MacIntyre sat down across the table and got to the point.

"We're having some difficulty with your statement," he said. "Now, I want to give you one last chance to tell us the truth."

"I've … I've told the truth," said Patricia.

"You've told some of the truth," said the officer. "But now we want it all. Do you know what perjury is, Patricia?"

"Perjury?"

"If you lie to us, you can go to jail. Did you know that?"

To Patricia, this was news. It also is not true. Giving false testimony under oath is punishable. Lying to police can be considered obstruction of justice but police would have to prove it. Still, the thought frightened Patricia.

"Jail?"

"Yes. This is a police investigation into a murder and it is as serious as it can get. Lying is not an option. Now, let's go back over what you remember from that evening."

"The night Sandy was stabbed?"

"Smart girl. Yes. You went to the dance."

"Yeah."

"And you and your boyfriend left before midnight."

"My boyfriend, that's Terry Gushue, he got in a fight and got kicked out of the dance. That's when we left. I got mad at him for drinking and fighting."

"And you met Donald Marshall?"

"First, we went to the park and sat on a bench and started arguing."

"Was anyone else there?"

"Robert Patterson came to the park with us. After a while we crossed the park behind the bandshell and went up to Crescent Street."

"Who did you see?"

"Junior Marshall. Terry got a match off him."

"Who was he with?"

"Junior? Two other men ..."

Detective MacIntyre slammed his fist into the table top. "No, Patricia. I don't want to hear any bullshit about two other men. There were no two other men. Tell us the truth!"

Startled by the outburst, Patricia jumped back in her chair. She felt tears forming.

"I'm telling …"

"You're not. We know you are not. Now tell the truth."

Patricia broke down in tears. Her mother reached out and comforted her.

MacIntyre signalled to one of the other officers and a glass of water appeared in front of Patricia. Her mother handed her a handkerchief.

"Can we try this again?" asked MacIntyre. "And we could do without the tears. Now, where were we? You met Junior Marshall. Terry got a light."

"And …" Patricia hesitated.

"Go on."

Patricia looked at her mother, who gave her hand a reassuring squeeze. But MacIntyre's eyes were hard.

"With Junior were two men," she began again, "and …"

Detective Urquhart crumpled a sheet of paper and threw it on the floor.

"We're going to drop that crap," said MacIntyre. "We know there were not two men in the park. That's something that Marshall himself cooked up. Now stop fooling around!"

"But I saw ..."

Urquhart crumpled more paper and swept it onto the floor.

Repeatedly, Patricia tried to relate her memory of the evening.

Finally, MacIntyre slammed his open palm on the table. "Enough, damn it! Come on, you didn't see two men. We're going to get the truth out of you. Do you understand? If we have to bring the full weight of the law down on you. If we have to send you to jail."

Patricia now broke down and sobbed.

Again her mother tried to comfort her. Patricia's sobs were the deep cries of pain and frustration of a child. Even her mother couldn't calm her down.

At last, MacIntyre came around the table and beckoned to Eunice Harriss, Patricia's mother.

"Ma'am, I'm asking you to leave the room for a bit."

"Leave? But ...?"

"She's not cooperating," he said. "Give us some time with her. Sometimes things work out best this way."

"Will ... will she be okay?"

Detective MacIntyre gave her a reassuring pat on the shoulder. "She's in good hands," he said, looking down at the tear-stained face of the fourteen-year-old girl.

Reluctantly, Eunice Harriss left the room.

Ideally, all minors were supposed to be accompanied by a parent when questioned by police. But this practice was commonly ignored.

"Now, let's get down to business," MacIntyre said. "And this time tell me the whole truth. Not any of that bullshit about two men."

"But the men were …"

"They weren't there! There were no men! You really want to spend some time in jail, don't you?"

Patricia sobbed. "I don't know what you want," she said, sucking up big sobs. One of the cops handed her a tissue to wipe her nose. "I tell you the truth and you yell …"

"It's not the truth! It's bullshit!" yelled MacIntyre.

The struggle between MacIntyre and the young teen continued for some time. Finally, MacIntyre left in a huff.

"Make yourself comfortable," he said from the doorway. "We plan to get the truth from you if it takes all night."

It was now well after midnight. Patricia was left alone in the room.

Being alone can be frightening. Just when she was beginning to feel really uncomfortable, the door opened and Terry Gushue, her boyfriend, came in.

"Hey," he said. "Don't cry. It's going to be okay."

"Yeah, but they keep yelling at me," she sniffed. The tissue in her hand had become soaked and useless.

"You'll be okay."

Patricia felt drained. She just wanted to go home. "Did you talk to them?" she asked Terry.

"I just told them we were together that night and that we saw Junior on Crescent Street with another man. That's when I got the light from him. That's it."

"That's all?"

"Well, it seemed to make them happy. Maybe that's what you should tell them. Just go along with what they want so you can go home."

"Just like that?"

"Just like that."

Terry left. Shortly after, MacIntyre and Urquhart re-entered the room.

"Okay, Patricia," said MacIntyre. "Can we start fresh now and get the truth? It's been a long day for everybody."

Patricia blinked back the remnants of her tears.

"Now, when you met Junior Marshall — that's what you called him — and Terry got a light, was there someone with him?"

"Yes."

"Who?"

"He had a dark jacket on."

"Was it Sandy Seale?"

"It looked like him."

"Did he speak to you?"

"No."

"Did Junior Marshall say anything else?"

"Not much."

"Was he drinking?"

"Yeah."

"Were they standing or walking when you met them?"

Patricia looked the officer in the eye.

"Well?"

"I'm not sure."

"Well, put it this way," said the officer. "Were they facing one another?"

"Yeah."

"When you came closer, did they move apart?"

"Yeah, Sandy moved back."

"That's all?"

"We talked to Junior, got a match, and left for home."

It was now 1:20 a.m. on June 18. The officers now treated her more kindly, and even smiled ever so slightly.

Only after she had signed the typed statement was she allowed to leave.

It had been hard work, but Sergeant of Detectives John MacIntyre had added one more statement that conformed to the events that appeared to make Donald Marshall guilty.

⋆   ⋆   ⋆

One person, Bob Patterson, appears in statements of several of the accounts. He was the young man so strung out on booze and drugs that he was vomiting in the flower beds at Wentworth Park that night. Donald Marshall claimed to be so concerned about him that he and Sandy Seale checked him out to see if he knew them. When Bob called them by name, they assumed he was okay. They hid him in a flower bed so police wouldn't find him.

Patricia Harriss mentioned him; Terry Gushue mentioned him. There could be no doubt that he was in the park at least prior to the stabbing. Police should have wanted to talk to him.

Both Detectives MacIntyre and Urquhart said they did try to find Patterson but couldn't. MacIntyre was not sure of the steps they took in the search. "I likely would have said to any of the fellows in the car (other police officers on patrol) if you see Bob Patterson, you know, pick him up and take him in. I want to talk to him."

MacIntyre later said he did not know Patterson — although he did know Patterson's mother by name (Geraldine) and where she lived (George Street).

Bob Patterson had a different story. He said a police car had picked him up and taken him to the station. He said MacIntyre and Urquhart grilled him, that MacIntyre had handcuffed him to a chair, banged his head on the table, and insisted that he had seen Marshall stab Seale. He said that Urquhart had produced a typed statement for him to sign — but refused to let him read it.

It is hard to believe that police could not find Bob Patterson in the small city of Sydney. Patterson was well known to police. In fact, in September 1971, Patterson spent some time in jail in Sydney. Surely police could have found him there.

But Patterson himself was a less-than-sterling witness. He had a lengthy criminal record and a vested interest in making police look bad. Besides, he was so drunk that night that Donald and Sandy both were worried about him. His memory would have been foggy at best.

CHAPTER THIRTEEN

LIES AND MORE LIES

On July 5, at his preliminary hearing, Donald and his lawyers got a first glimpse of the twisted stories of friends.

A preliminary hearing is usually a formality — an occasion for the Crown to show that there is enough evidence to make a trial worthwhile. It was held in the courthouse, less than a block from the scene of the stabbing.

In practice, defence lawyers get to see the case the Crown has prepared, as well as some hint of the evidence.

That strategy became clear to Donald right away, even without legal training. The first witness, Patricia Harriss, told of meeting Donald and Sandy the night of the stabbing. But she made no mention of seeing the other two men (Jimmy MacNeil and Roy Ebsary). If she had, the case against Donald would have been weakened.

Later, Donald sat in stunned disbelief as Maynard

Chant told a story of standing on train tracks and watching Donald take a knife from his pocket and stab Sandy Seale.

Then John Pratico told a similar story of hiding behind a bush between the railway tracks and Crescent Street, and seeing Donald Marshall stab Sandy Seale.

By the end of the day, Donald knew his troubles were serious: three people had lied. He could not figure out why.

And without any legal training, with only six years of completed education, he could predict the result: he would be tried in court for the murder of Sandy Seale.

And now he knew he had reason to be worried.

★   ★   ★

Four months later, on November 2, 1971, five months and four days after the death of Sandy Seale, Donald Marshall Jr. went on trial. The judge for the case was Mr. Justice J. Louis Dubinsky.

Anyone accused of a serious crime has the right to be tried by a jury of peers. "Peers" means equals. A jury is picked from people of the same mix of race, national origin, and gender as the population at large. But attitudes of more than forty years ago in Cape Breton were different. It did not surprise Donald when the jury, selected from a pool of fifty, ended up being twelve white men.

Many in the Mi'kmaw community were also dismayed that the Crown prosecutor was Donald MacNeil. MacNeil was a powerful lawyer. But like many others in Nova Scotia (and in other parts of Canada) during the 1970s, his attitude about race were deeply buried. People often held racist beliefs without knowing they were racist. And MacNeil had previously had his wrists slapped for racist comments in court.

The testimony from the preliminary hearing had been damning. Two witnesses testified to seeing Donald stab Sandy. A third, Patricia Harriss, told of seeing Donald and Sandy in the park — but no one else. Despite a publication ban on the preliminary hearing, word had spread. It was little wonder that public sentiment was against Donald. Sandy's family and the black community in general were irate and turned up to see a killer convicted.

Defending Donald should have been easy: find holes in the lies of the key witnesses and squeeze out the truth. Donald knew he had told the truth. What he did not realize at this time, however, were the legal barriers now in front of him.

The biggest of these challenges was the lack of full disclosure. Usually, Crown prosecutors would let defence lawyers see all the evidence before the trial. If Donald's lawyers
had asked, they likely would have been given the earlier
police statements by Patricia Harriss, Maynard Chant, and
John Pratico. But in 1971, the laws of Nova Scotia did not
demand full disclosure. And Donald's lawyers did not ask.

All Donald knew as he watched from the prisoner's
box was that three people had lied.

Despite the stakes, Donald found the hearing boring.
He tuned out. It was a parade: Detective MacDonald, the
doctor at the hospital, the Seale family, and the lawyers
jawing back and forth about what could and could not
be talked about. To Donald, all of it was confusing. He
called it "white words."

One early witness did jar him. The Crown tried to
show that Donald had cut himself on the arm to make
his story believable. The nurse from the hospital told the
jury that the wound on his arm did not bleed. That didn't
bother Donald — he knew it had bled. But before she
left the stand, she was asked one final question.

"Did you notice anything else about his arm?"

"I noticed the tattoo on his arm," she replied.

"What part of the arm was that on?" asked the Crown
attorney.

"On the outer aspect of his arm."

"Can you tell us what that tattoo is?"

Donald held his breath waiting for the answer.

"I hate cops," the nurse replied.

The looks on the faces of the jury members frightened Donald.

His arm, and the wound on it, caused even more concern. At the preliminary hearing, the doctor who had put the stitches in his wound had been clear: the wound was not self-inflicted, but it could have been.

But now, the doctor changed his story. He was asked by the Crown attorney if the wound "had the appearance of being self-inflicted."

"It's possible," the doctor replied.

The small difference in wording was important. The first version the jury heard suggested the wound was possibly self-inflicted. Donald's lawyers tried to undo that picture but feared the jury would remember only key points: "wound ... self-inflicted."

Such a sea of words confused Donald. At times, he found he could daydream through them. But when fourteen-year-old Patricia Harriss took the stand again, he refocused. This was the girl he and Sandy had chatted to briefly that night; he had lit her cigarette, briefly holding her hand to steady the match. Now she seemed ready to repeat the lies she had told at the preliminary hearing.

Donald was delighted when her story changed.

Asked what time she had left the dance, Patricia said that she and Terry Gushue left "about ten-thirty."

"What did you do at ten-thirty?" asked the Crown attorney.

"Well, my boyfriend was asked to leave the dance, so I went with him down to Wentworth Park, in front of the bandshell, and we stayed there for a while. First we got a package of cigarettes. We went down and sat on the bench. A friend walked by and we asked him for a match, and he lit the cigarette. After that, we left and went to Crescent Street."

She added that after sitting to smoke a cigarette, she and Terry continued into the park. Not far from the site of the stabbing, they got a light from Donald Marshall.

Donald sat up in his chair. *This would be about eleven p.m., then. She was an hour out on the time. An hour before the stabbing.*

Even Donald knew that this made her story if not obviously untrue, worthless in proving his guilt. His hopes began to rise.

Next on the stand was Terry Gushue. Similar to Patricia, he said they had left the dance at about 10:30 p.m. He said that shortly before 11 p.m. they had met

Donald Marshall. There was someone with Donald, he said, but he could not say who this was. Donald gave him a match, and they left for home.

Donald realized that Terry's story supported what Patricia had said. That hour didn't prove his innocence, but it did mean that what Patricia and Terry said didn't mean much at all. He hoped the jurors would see this, too.

★   ★   ★

When Maynard Chant came to the stand, Donald fixed his eyes on him, trying to stare him down. Maynard looked away.

Right away, the lawyers argued about stuff that Donald didn't understand. Finally, the judge ruled that while Maynard was testifying, other witnesses would have to wait outside. That included John Pratico, who left his seat in the courtroom to wait in the hallway.

Donald turned his attention to Maynard on the stand.

Maynard repeated the lie he trotted out at the preliminary hearing: being on the railroad tracks, seeing someone hiding behind a bush (likely John Pratico?), looking back to see two people arguing near the bridge, and seeing one guy take something from his pocket and "drive it towards the other fellow's stomach."

Donald realized this was a mildly different version of the lie that Maynard had told at the preliminary hearing. But he noted the key difference: in July, Maynard had said clearly that he saw Donald do the stabbing with a knife. Now, the story had changed to simply one guy jabbing something into the stomach of another. It was still a lie but half a degree softer.

"Did you recognize either of these two gentlemen?" asked Crown Attorney MacNeil, trying to get Maynard to pin the stabbing directly on Donald.

"No, sir."

Maynard said he then ran down the tracks to Bentinck Street to get to the bus terminal. "I saw a fellow running towards me," he said. "He caught up with me and by that time I recognized him and it was a Marshall — Marshall fellow."

This was not the same story he told at the preliminary hearing. He was saying that he saw who stabbed Sandy, but didn't recognize him. Then, minutes later, he saw Donald.

Donald wasn't quite sure what the change in his story meant. One of his lawyers indicated that it should mean a lot. It was a strange testimony. Of course, Maynard hadn't seen anything at all.

Donald's lawyers said they thought the Crown attorney was having trouble keeping the stories of his young witnesses straight.

14

CHAPTER FOURTEEN

SECOND THOUGHTS

After he was sent into the hallway to wait, John Pratico was nervous.

It was November 3, the second day of the trial. Outside, a gusty wind tossed the last leaves from the trees. Even in the corridor of the courtroom, he could feel the chill of the draft.

I can't do it, he thought, slumping with his back to the wall.

At the preliminary hearing back in July, he had repeated the statement he had given to police on June 4 — his second statement — that he had seen the stabbing.

There was no doubt in John's mind that his testimony had helped put Donald on trial. Now, he was in a bind.

First, that statement was a lie. He had not seen the stabbing.

Police had told him over and over again that he had to repeat his story one more time at the trial. If he did not, he was told, he would be guilty of perjury and could be sent to jail.

But now that the trial had begun, the seriousness began to sink in: Donald Marshall was on trial for murder. If he was found guilty, he could be sent to jail for life.

For life!

Pratico's lies could help send Junior to jail. But what should he do about it?

Back in July, at the preliminary hearing, John Pratico had said he had seen Marshall stab Sandy Seale.

But word on the street had taken its toll. In the small world of Sydney, the teenagers who were witnesses, and even undoubtedly others who had simply been at the dance that night, compared notes. Many had seen John Pratico at the dance. He was drunk. Some helped half carry him to the nearby lumberyard to sleep it off. That's where he was at the time of the stabbing. He had to be lying.

Now, minutes before he was to be called to testify one last time, Pratico may have realized that this was no longer a game. In the hallway outside the courtroom, he approached Donald Marshall Sr. — Junior's father.

"He didn't do it," John Pratico said.

Donald Sr. turned.

"Say what?" he replied.

"He didn't do it," John repeated. "Junior didn't kill nobody."

Donald Sr. could not believe his ears.

"You testified at the preliminary hearing," he said. "You said ..."

"I lied. I didn't see nobody do no stabbing."

"Then why did you say so?"

"The police, they wanted me to say that. They kept pushing me to say it. They said I'd go to jail."

Donald Sr. spun on his heels.

"Don't go away," he said. "Maybe it's not too late."

It should not have been too late. John Pratico had not yet testified. Donald Marshall Sr. pushed through the crowd and up to Simon Khattar, one of his son's defence lawyers, in a break from proceedings.

"Pratico just told me he didn't see a thing," he said. "He says police threatened to send him to jail."

Immediately, Khattar summoned the High Sheriff for the county of Cape Breton. The sheriff in turn summoned Crown Attorney Donald MacNeil. Several others were also summoned, including Moe Rosenblum (Marshall's other lawyer) and Detective John MacIntyre.

And, finally, John Pratico.

In the lawyers' lounge at the courthouse, John repeated his story: he had not seen Marshall stab Seale. But he was worried about perjury. Police had told him that if he changed his story, he would be guilty of perjury and could go to jail.

Everyone at that meeting advised John Pratico to tell the truth when he took the witness stand and not to be concerned about perjury.

What happened next sealed the fate of Donald Marshall Jr.

As soon as Pratico was sworn in as a witness, Crown Attorney MacNeil tried to introduce the evidence of what had been said outside the courtroom.

The judge refused to hear it, and ordered MacNeil to question his witness on the events on the night of the murder. So despite his attempts at honesty, Pratico found himself nudged to repeat his fabrication told in July: hiding behind a bush near the railroad tracks, he had seen Donald Marshall take a knife from his pocket and stab Sandy Seale.

"Did you recognize them at the time?"

"Yes."

"What, if anything, did you see them do?"

"Well, they stood there for a while talking and arguing, and then Marshall's hand come out, his right hand come out like this —." He tried to show the movement.

He again repeated his line about the object.

"What did he do with the shiny object?"

"Plunged it into Seale's stomach."

"What did Seale do?"

"He fell. And that's the last I seen."

After an overnight break, Pratico returned to the stand the next morning.

In cross-examination, Simon Khattar tried to establish for the jury how drunk this seventh-grade student had been.

"Were you sick at the dance on May 28?" Khattar asked.

"Liquor-sick, yes."

"Were you taken into the washroom and given some help by some of your friends?" the lawyer asked.

"Yes."

Later, Khattar came back to the same point. "Did I understand you earlier in your evidence to say that you had been drinking on that day, this is, May 28 of this year?"

"Yes, sir."

"What did you first drink that evening?"

"I think it was wine," Pratico replied. He said he had drunk half a bottle of wine before changing to beer.

"Beer. How much beer did you drink?"

"Maybe half a dozen quarts I drank. And pints."

"Half a dozen quarts and how many pints?"

"Two or three," the youth answered.

"Did you drink anything else?"

Pratico said he had but could not recall if it had been rum, vodka, or gin.

He recalled leaving the dance, but didn't know what time it was and could not remember if he had been alone.

Later, Donald's lawyer brought Pratico back to his final switch in his story. Khattar asked Pratico to repeat his eyewitness account: "I seen Mr. Marshall's hand come out like this here and go towards Mr. Seale's stomach, and that's all I seen."

Then the lawyer switched gears.

He brought John Pratico back to the conversation in the hallway and barristers' lounge the previous afternoon. Carefully, he asked John to list those who had been present: himself, the defence lawyer, the sheriff. He then asked John to repeat what he had said:

"I said that Mr. Marshall didn't stab Mr. Seale."

But before he could go much further, Judge Dubinsky interrupted. He ordered Khattar to limit himself to questions about the difference between what Pratico said at the preliminary hearing and what he was saying now at the trial.

The judge had smothered the last-minute attempt by the troubled teen to tell the truth.

15

CHAPTER FIFTEEN

DONALD TESTIFIES

When Donald Marshall took the witness stand in his own defence, he was scared.

The faces in the courtroom frightened him. Sandy Seale's family sat together, but their eyes were filled with hate. Already they had branded him as guilty. That hurt him.

A few friendly faces helped him: his father, a brother, and other members from Membertou. But as always, they were a minority.

But from the bench, the judge peered down at him through lowered glasses. Crown Attorney MacNeil almost shook the floor when he walked. And right in the front row, Sergeant of Detectives John MacIntyre sat with his arms folded and a smirk on his face.

One on one, Donald loved to talk with almost anyone. But he had no experience speaking in public. Shy and often inarticulate, Donald stumbled over his words. It didn't help that even his own lawyer kept bugging him, asking him to not cover his mouth when he spoke. It reminded him of school, like a teacher ordering him not to mumble. His last day in school had not ended well. And court felt like school — only worse.

He did his best to tell what had actually happened that night: that two drunks had bummed cigarettes and had given a racial taunt — and then the older guy stabbed Sandy

Even with his own lawyer, Donald showed his nervousness. Repeatedly, his own lawyer asked him to move his hand away from his mouth so he could be heard.

Under cross-examination, it was worse. Crown Attorney MacNeil made fun of Donald's testimony.

Why didn't he seek help immediately, MacNeil asked. "Did these two men attempt to follow you?"

"I started running," Donald replied. He recalled the terror of that night, his fear.

"You started running?" asked MacNeil.

"Yes."

"Did they attempt to follow you?"

Donald explained that the two men ran behind a house. He didn't feel he had to explain why he ran. He knew: fear.

"Why did you not go to a house to seek aid, assist-ance?" asked the Crown attorney.

For once, Donald's answer was crystal clear. "I wasn't going to take a chance on going back," he said. "By the time somebody comes up, I'm liable to be dead."

After the stabbing when he returned to the scene, MacNeil suggested Donald had kept his back to Sandy Seale.

"You stood there in such a position that he could not see you, isn't that correct?"

It was an accusation meant to influence the jury. It was so absurd that Donald could not answer.

Later in the cross-examination, even the judge jumped in, suggesting that Donald had gone to John Pratico's house to threaten him.

"Did you say you went to see Pratico on Saturday?" the judge asked.

"I went by his house. I met him on the step," Donald replied.

"On Sunday?" said the judge.

"Yeah."

The judge asked if he had been at Pratico's house on Saturday afternoon.

"Yeah."

"And Sunday?"

"And Sunday evening," Donald replied.

"Where did you meet him?"

"His house."

"Inside?"

"No."

"Outside?"

"Yes," Donald replied.

The web of questions would later suggest that Donald had sought out Pratico to threaten him — that Donald knew he had seen the stabbing.

In the cross-examination about the stabbing, the judge jumped in again.

"Mr. Marshall," said the judge. "I didn't get what you said. You saw two men. Two men, and one asked for a cigarette?"

"Yeah."

"Speak up."

"Yes."

Donald testified that the older of the two drunks said they were from Manitoba. "I said, 'you look like priests,'" he added.

"Then what did the younger man say?" asked the judge.

"'We are,'" Donald replied.

"Then what?"

"Pardon?" asked Donald, confused.

"Who went on to say that they didn't like —"

"Coloured people," Donald replied.

"The younger or older?" asked Judge Dubinsky.

"The older," replied Donald.

"The older man said what?"

"We don't like niggers."

The judge looked down over his glasses. "'We don't like niggers or Indians,'" the judge repeated. "That's the older man [who] said that?"

"Yeah."

"And then what happened?"

"He took out a knife and he drove it into Seale's stomach."

The judge repeated the point.

"And turned on me," Donald added.

The judge repeated this, too, as though making notes.

"Swung the knife at me," Donald said.

The judge repeated again.

"I moved my arm. He cut me in the left arm."

After a short break, Judge Dubinsky asked more questions about Pratico. The judge seemed to want to fix that idea in the minds of the jurors: that Donald knew Pratico had seen the stabbing and wanted to threaten him. But since Pratico's story was a fabrication built on the facts

Donald had described, it was hard to refute.

In summing up the case, the defence had little to go on but the truth. Donald knew that despite having the truth on his side, he had not been a strong witness. The Crown, on the other hand, argued that Maynard Chant and John Pratico told essentially the same story, and they didn't know about each other. This meant they must both be telling the truth. That was it then, Donald thought. The "white" way — two lies make a truth?

He listened in despair at Crown Attorney MacNeil's final words to the jury: "They (the Crown and police) have given you the best evidence that you could possibly get and that's an eyewitness. Not one eyewitness but two eyewitnesses, and I suggest to you that the Crown has discharged its obligation and it is your duty — bound under the oath that you took for office — to find the accused guilty as charged."

After MacNeil finished his summation, court was adjourned late in the afternoon of November 4. All that remained was for the judge to address the jury.

★   ★   ★

That night, Barbara Floyd called Rosenblum's law office. Barbara was one of the teens at the dance the night of the stabbing and had provided some testimony to corroborate other witnesses.

She had read the story in the newspaper about Pratico's testimony and decided it must be false. At the time the stabbing took place, she was one of a group with John Pratico.

"Can I speak to Donald Marshall's lawyers?" she said into the phone.

There was a pause.

A man came back on the line.

"Can I help you?"

"Yeah, I had just read the paper and am calling about John Pratico," she said.

"What about him?"

"He couldn't possibly be a witness because he was at the dance. He ..."

She didn't get to say much more.

"You're too late," he said.

"I beg your pardon?"

"You're too late," the voice repeated and hung up.

Once more, a valid attempt to bring truth to the trial failed. It would not be the last time.

★   ★   ★

The next morning in his summation, Judge Dubinsky focused the attention of the jury on the two key witnesses, Chant and Pratico. Essentially, it came down to whom the jury would believe: Chant and Pratico or Donald Marshall. And as a judge will do, he made it clear that only the jury could make a decision about the facts — which witnesses to believe.

He added: "In my opinion, there is not the slightest suggestion in this case that Maynard Chant was in collusion with John Pratico."

The implication was clear: either they had gotten together to tell the same lie or they were telling the truth. And he said there was nothing to suggest they got together.

Then he sent the jury out to come to a decision.

*   *   *

At 12:40 p.m., the jury retired to consider their verdict. Less than four hours later the all-white, all-male jury returned to say they had found Marshall guilty.

At 4:45 p.m. on November 5, 1971, Justice Dubinsky asked Donald to stand while he pronounced sentence:

"The sentence of the court is that you, Donald Marshall Jr., shall be imprisoned in Dorchester Penitentiary in

Dorchester, New Brunswick, subject to the rules and regulations of that institution, for life."

At first, Donald, by then eighteen, could not understand what the words meant. They made no sense. He felt lost. When the reality hit him, he cried the tears of childhood.

16

CHAPTER SIXTEEN

JIMMY CAN'T SLEEP

Jimmy MacNeil had not been sleeping well that summer.

The conviction of Donald Marshall Jr. for murder did not help.

The incident in the park had disturbed him. *Sure, he had been drunk that night. But he still remembered. In fact, that was the problem: he could not forget.*

He and Roy Ebsary had spent the night drinking, first some wine at home, then in a pub. He had been drunk; there was no way around that.

He remembered he and Roy bumming cigarettes off two kids, the black kid and the Indian.

And then the stabbing.

Roy had just lashed out, stabbing one, slashing at the other. One ran away. The other didn't; he just lay there. They left him groaning in a spreading pool of blood.

He had gone along with Roy's request and hadn't said

*anything; Roy had a wife and two daughters, and Jimmy didn't
want to get him in trouble.*

Still.

By November, Jimmy's mother knew that something was wrong. He was twenty-five, still living at
home. And now the sleepless nights, the walking, walking, walking.

Finally, she sat him down in the kitchen.

"What's going on?"

"What do you mean?"

"Something's not right," said his mother. "What's
bothering you? You can't fool a mother."

Jimmy, a labourer when he could find work, finally
broke his self-imposed code of silence.

"That Indian is in jail for something he did not do,"
Jimmy said. "It isn't fair." He told about the events in
Wentworth Park that had been in the news only the
week before.

Once the story was out, Jimmy found it easier. His
mother insisted he tell his brother, Johnnie.

Johnnie had one reply: "You gotta go to the police,"
he said.

He did.

On November 15, ten days after Donald Marshall Jr.
had been convicted of murder, Jimmy MacNeil walked

into the Sydney police department. His brother Johnnie was with him.

"That Indian didn't do it," he told police. "I was there. Roy Ebsary stabbed that kid."

This was something that police could not ignore.

Later that evening, Jimmy MacNeil, accompanied by his brothers Johnnie and David, sat in an interview room at police headquarters.

"Okay," said the officer. "Let's start at the beginning. Your name?"

"James William MacNeil."

"Age?"

"Twenty-five."

"Address?"

"1007 Rear George Street, Sydney."

"So for the record now, tell us what happened. That night of May 28."

Jimmy exchanged glances with his two brothers. His fingers shook as he lit a cigarette.

"Myself and Roy Ebsary were at the State Tavern. George Street, Sydney. We were there about an hour or so. We left."

"And?"

"We walked down George Street and took the short-cut through the park. We came up to Crescent Street and were approached by an Indian and a coloured fellow from behind.

"The Indian put my right hand up behind my back. The coloured fellow said, 'Dig, man, dig.' Then Roy Ebsary said, 'I got something for you.' He put his hand in his right pocket and took out a knife and drove it into the coloured fellow's side."

"What side?"

"The left-hand side of the coloured fellow. I seen Roy's hand and knife full of blood."

"Did you see the Indian being stabbed?"

"No, I did not."

"What happened then?"

Again, Jimmy exchanged glances with his brothers. "Roy went home and I went with him. He washed the knife under the tap and washed his hands off. Then he told me not to say anything about it."

"Did you ask him why he had done it?"

"Yes, he said it was self-defence."

"What time did you get home that night?"

"About twelve p.m."

"How long were you at Roy's house that night?"

"About an hour after that."

"When did you see Roy again?"

"The next day I went to his house. He was laying

[sick] in bed. I told him that fellow died."

"What did he say?"

"He said it was self-defence. I told him he did not have to kill him. He told me he had two children — a girl and a boy — and not to say anything to the police. I left then."

"Who saw you at the house besides Roy?"

"His wife, daughter, and son."

"Did they say anything to you?"

"No. Not that day. About two days after that, his son, about eighteen or nineteen years old, came to my house with his car. He drove me out to the Wandlyn Motel. He went in the motel and his mother came out to the car. She got in the back seat. He got in and she said, 'Don't go to their house anymore,' because of what Roy had done. The young fellow told me if I mentioned what happened to police, all your family will be in trouble. They will have to go to court."

The police officer wrote more notes, then continued. "What were you wearing that night?"

"I was wearing a college coat, blue with two white marks on the sleeve." Jimmy had been proud of that jacket. Though he had never attended college, he had picked it up the year before but could not remember where.

"What was Roy wearing?"

"A black shawl over his shoulders, something like a priest wears over his shoulders."

"When did you tell someone about this?"

"The first one I told was my mother. She noticed I was not sleeping and was walking around since the last trial. She asked me, and I told her 'bout the stabbing and that the Indian man was in jail for something he did not do. It wasn't fair. Then I told my brother Johnnie last night. He told me to go to the police."

"Did you know Marshall or Seale?"

"No."

Almost immediately, police swung into action. That same day, statements were taken from Roy Ebsary, his wife, Mary, and their son, Greg. All three were invited to police headquarters. All gave statements.

Ebsary's daughter, Donna, thirteen years old, sat outside the police station in the family car while statements were taken from the rest of her family. Perhaps police thought that she was too young. It was another police oversight that could have changed the outcome of the case.

Her story did not fully emerge for sixteen years.

★　★　★

Two days after Jimmy MacNeil gave his statement to Sydney police, the RCMP took charge. Detective Inspector Alan Marshall (no relation to Donald) was assigned to determine whether MacNeil's story meant anything.

But the Donald Marshall Jr. story bulges with bungling.

The RCMP investigation relied heavily on the files of the Sydney police — the same investigation under Sergeant of Detectives John MacIntyre that saw Donald convicted.

For one thing, RCMP Detective Inspector Marshall never had the entire file on the case. He didn't even ask for it. Because of that, he had no way of knowing of all the witness statements and contradictions.

He did re-interview Jimmy MacNeil and concluded his story "was a figment of his imagination." (Detective MacIntyre had apparently told him that MacNeil's was a "cock and bull story," and shared his theory that Donald Marshall Jr.'s wound was self-inflicted.)

The RCMP had more resources than the Sydney police. This enabled Detective Inspector Marshall to have lie-detector tests administered to both Roy Ebsary and Jimmy MacNeil.

The lie detector, or polygraph, often used in law

enforcement is considered unreliable. In this case, its results matched its reputation. The RCMP officer who administered the tests said they showed that Roy Ebsary was telling the truth when he said he had not stabbed Sandy Seale. He said he could give no opinion on Jimmy MacNeil.

Without re-interviewing any of the key witnesses, Detective Inspector Marshall relied on the polygraph tests and one interview with Jimmy MacNeil. At no time had the Crown attorney let Donald Marshall's defence lawyers know about Jimmy MacNeil's story and the polygraph tests. Obviously, he believed MacIntyre. He squandered a chance to reveal the truth.

On December 21, RCMP officer Marshall filed a report that said he had conducted "a thorough review of the case" and concluded that Donald Marshall Jr. had stabbed Sandy Seale.

Merry Christmas, Donald.

CHAPTER SEVENTEEN

LAWYERS APPEAL

The day after Jimmy MacNeil arrived at the Sydney police headquarters to tell his revised story, Donald Marshall Jr.'s lawyer filed a notice to appeal. There was no connection between the two events. In fact, Donald's lawyers didn't know about Jimmy MacNeil's new story.

If they had, the appeal would likely have ended on a happier note.

In the appeal, Moe Rosenblum listed twelve reasons for the conviction to be overturned.

At least eight of the reasons cited errors made by Mr. Justice J. Louis Dubinsky in the original trial. He claimed that the "Learned Trial Judge" didn't properly inform the jury about the defence case, misdirected the jury, and was biased.

He also claimed that the conviction was not supported by the evidence.

The appeal system is designed to correct errors made

by the system. In general, an appeal can be made only on points of law. An exception can be made for new evidence that would cast the verdict in doubt.

John Pratico's change of heart at the last minute of the trial should have raised warning flags. Had Donald's lawyer raised that issue in the appeal, a new trial would likely have been ordered.

In short, Rosenblum had plenty of ammunition to argue for a new trial. He just didn't load the right cartridges and fired blanks instead. Usually known as a diligent lawyer, he appeared to be just going through the motions. It is possible he did not believe that Donald was innocent. One court worker in Sydney at the time would later say that he thought Rosenblum "did not work as hard for Native clients."

The Court of Appeal itself had the power to review the whole case. It could have dealt with the issues on its own — not that it had a duty to do so, said one law professor, but it "would be a proper exercise in discretion" — a moral duty.

As mentioned earlier, the Crown attorney had once been chided for racist comments. The jury itself included no minorities of any kind. Donald's lawyers perhaps didn't work as hard for aboriginal clients.

The appeal failed. Donald still faced life in prison.

Could it get worse?

During his time in prison, Donald protested his innocence as loudly as possible. His father rattled whatever cages
he could. Throughout the whole ordeal, Donald Marshall
Sr. had supported his son. He believed in his innocence.

The case had cost the Marshall family dearly. Even
before the trial, public opinion had been against Donald.
The Marshall family phone was flooded with threatening calls. The family changed to an unlisted number. But
Chief Marshall's plastering business depended on the
phone. With the number changed, business calls dried
up; he lost the business.

Then, in 1974, after Donald had spent three years in
prison, a glimmer of hope shone in the dark. Another
witness emerged.

Right after the trial, Jimmy MacNeil had tried to tell
police that Roy Ebsary had stabbed Sandy Seale. That's
when police interviewed three of the four members of
the Ebsary family. One member of the Ebsary family was
left out.

While Roy, his common-law wife, and son, Greg,
gave statements to police, Roy's daughter, Donna, thirteen, remained outside in the car. It was just one more
oversight by police; she was the one member of the
family, besides her father, who had a story to tell.

The night of the murder she had seen her father washing what she thought was blood off a knife. She believed her father had killed Sandy Seale.

The story might never have come to light except for coincidence — or perhaps simply because Sydney is a small community. Donna was studying martial arts from instructor David Ratchford. They became friends. Eventually, she shared her story with David.

David was also friends with Constable Gary Green of the Sydney RCMP. At David Ratchford's urging, Donna told Green about her father and the knife and the blood. Constable Green in turn told them to go to the Sydney police with the story. He even accompanied them. Donna told her story to Detective William Urquhart.

But Urquhart — who had been the second-in-command in the original investigation — didn't believe the tale.

Donna Ebsary was "a disturbed and disgruntled young lady," Urquhart said, and he was not going to reconsider the matter based on another rumour. The matter, he said, had already been reviewed by the RCMP.

Matter closed.

It would not stay closed, however. Donald Marshall's conviction was like a meal that the Nova Scotia legal system could not digest; it kept coming back up, time and time again.

18

CHAPTER EIGHTEEN

BRIEF FREEDOM

Three years into his life sentence, Donald did something he never thought he would do: he admitted to killing Sandy Seale.

It wasn't the truth, of course. His behaviour in the maximum security at Dorchester was sterling. Still, his application for transfer to the minimum security in Springhill, Nova Scotia, was long overdue. After witnessing beatings and a murder, he knew he had to get out of Dorchester. The first step to rehabilitation required a prisoner to accept that he had done wrong. This Donald had refused to do.

But his classification officers made it clear that without admitting guilt, he would spend his life, literally, behind bars.

So he told officials he had killed Sandy Seale.

It worked. A few weeks later, on Halloween in 1974,

he received news of his transfer to Springhill. Four days later, three years to the day after a jury had found him guilty, he was transferred.

Life in Springhill was easier. Within the institution, inmates had access to the library, the gym, and school. Donald completed grade ten, joined Alcoholics Anonymous, became a native leader, and started running for fitness.

Although he had made an ideal adjustment to Springhill, his "confession" did not sit well with him. In the spring of 1975, he recanted and told his classification officer that he had confessed simply to get to Springhill. He insisted that he had not killed Sandy Seale.

Over the next few months, his applications for day parole, or any kind of pass outside of Springhill, were turned down. When his grandmother died, his application for a temporary leave of absence was turned down. The reason? The chief of police of Sydney said he feared for the lives of witnesses if Donald came home even for a short time. The chief by that time was John MacIntyre — the same officer who had bullied witnesses to lie.

In 1978, seven years into his sentence, Donald got a taste of freedom with a camping trip forty-eight kilometres into the wilderness. He and five other inmates camped, fished, and swam in the clean waters under the freedom of the sky in rural Nova Scotia.

But it was only a taste, and he wanted more.

In 1979, about a year after his first camping trip, Donald heard about a week-long canoe trip of the Native Brotherhood Canoeing Expedition. He applied. He continued his physical training program. Included in that was having a cast removed on a broken wrist — the result of a fight in a prison floor-hockey game with a six-foot-four, 220-pound tough guy. Donald won the fight but suffered a broken wrist.

For the second part of his plan, Donald needed cash.

He watched carefully at the regular poker games. Experienced inmates worked in pairs to fleece newcomers. Donald watched the games in progress for a while and was able to figure out the system.

In one session, he fleeced the fleecers and won more than eight hundred dollars.

He needed the money. He planned to escape.

The scheme was simple: on the way back from the camping trip, he would slip away. By doing so on the way back, he would not endanger the ten-day camping trip. He didn't want his sponsor and his fellow prisoners on the trip to suffer.

Originally, the return trip called for an overnight stay in Truro, Nova Scotia. A friend would meet him in Truro when the group stopped at a motel. The friend would drive him to British Columbia, where the two would work in a lumber camp. There, he figured, he could blend in and not be noticed.

But on the way back from the camping trip, the guard stopped for lunch in Alma, Nova Scotia. Donald and the prisoners filled up on coffee and lemon meringue pie. The guard then announced a change of plans: instead of stopping overnight in Truro, he said, he would top up the gas tank, and they would return to Springhill that night.

Donald had to act quickly.

Leaving his coffee steaming on the table, Donald nodded in return to the brief salute of his fellow prisoners. While the guard filled the tank, Marshall sauntered towards the rest room at the back of the service station. He ducked behind a trailer and took off on a flat-out sprint.

His path took him through a mile or more of bog — not the easiest ground to cover. The mud sucked at his feet and brush scratched his legs. He changed his clothes, but by mistake threw away his maps, address book, and money.

By mid-afternoon, he saw the RCMP plane in the sky. At the same time the police had spotted him.

For the next five hours, the plane circled overhead. Donald hid under the branches of trees and waited. Finally, near dark, he resumed his journey.

He emerged on the highway near the Michelin plant at Granton, Nova Scotia. He had covered about seven kilometres.

Evading the police roadblocks, he hitched a ride in the Michelin parking lot as workers changed shifts. Seven kilometres later, he stepped out onto the street in Pictou, only blocks from his girlfriend's apartment.

Donald had met Shelly Sarson three years earlier. Shelly had been visiting her brother in Dorchester.

Now he surprised her. But she didn't think it was a good idea. "They'll kill you," she said. "Turn yourself in."

Donald refused and finally Shelly agreed to join him on the run.

The lovers had two days together, planning a life on the lam. But while Shelly stepped out to say goodbye to her mother, two RCMP cars arrived. Four officers stomped into the small apartment. They found Donald Marshall Jr. hiding in a closet.

With a twelve-gauge shotgun levelled at his chest, Donald ignored the command to give up. Then, from a crib behind the Mountie, Shelly's two-year-old niece stood up to see what the fuss was about.

Donald later said that he didn't want the child to see them picking pieces of him off the walls.

Donald stepped out of the closet and surrendered.

CHAPTER NINETEEN

DONALD FINDS THE KILLER

Shelly Sarson also figured largely in the coincidence that gave Donald one final glimmer of hope after ten years in prison.

In 1976, Shelly had been visiting her brother, John, at Dorchester prison. Donald noticed her. The sparks were mutual, and though separated by prison walls, the two fell in love.

Despite the odds against them, and the frightening events of Donald's attempted escape, the two were still a couple five years after they first met.

Donald's behaviour in Springhill had finally caught up to him, and again on Halloween night in 1980, he was transferred back to maximum security in Dorchester.

In August 1981, Shelly visited Donald at Dorchester. This time, she brought a second brother, Mitchell.

They chatted for a while before Mitchell asked

Donald if he knew a guy named Roy Ebsary. Donald said he did not know the man.

Mitchell knew Roy, and had one time even lived at Ebsary's house.

Then Mitchell said something that Donald had wanted to hear for more than ten years: that Roy Ebsary once told him he had killed a black guy and stabbed an Indian in Wentworth Park in 1971.

Donald was stunned.

He now had the name of the man who stabbed Sandy Seale. All he had to do was prove it, and he would be a free man.

Wouldn't he?

Donald swung into action. He renewed his efforts to have his case examined one more time. He hired a young lawyer, Stephen Aronson, who first visited him at Dorchester only a few days after Shelly's visit.

Mitchell Sarson repeated his story for the lawyer and for a couple of the council members from Membertou. For the first time since that horrid night in May 1971, things were looking up.

Without even much hope of payment, lawyer Aronson began to build a case for an appeal. He built the case slowly and carefully.

Mitchell Sarson's story had one flaw: his sister was

Marshall's girlfriend. Could the story about Ebsary be one the two cooked up to free Donald? Working alone, without pay for months and neglecting other parts of his law practice, Aronson reviewed the trial transcript. He dug into the case.

He found that Ebsary had been involved in other knife incidents.

He wrote to John MacIntyre asking that the case be reopened.

MacIntyre was now Chief of Police in Sydney. When he received the letter, he turned the matter over to the RCMP.

This time, the Mounties dug a little deeper.

20

CHAPTER TWENTY

THE WHEATON INVESTIGATION

The RCMP investigation landed on the desk of Staff
Sergeant Harry Wheaton. He was plain-clothes coordin-
ator of the General Investigation Section of the Sydney
RCMP.

Tall, good looking, with blue eyes, Wheaton had
grown up in farm country in New Brunswick. He had
buried his childhood dream of being an airline pilot and
joined the RCMP.

Early in his career, he received honours for bravery
after he risked his life to save the life of a man overcome
by gas fumes at the bottom of a well. He tackled under-
cover assignments in Montreal and Toronto, and later
took over Sydney's drug section — and was known as
"Dirty Harry" for his tough investigations.

He proved to be the ideal man for the job.

Wheaton reviewed the original statements provided

by MacIntyre as well as the trial transcript and the 1971 RCMP review. He interviewed Roy Ebsary's wife, Mary. He talked to Jimmy MacNeil and Mitchell Sarson.

Still skeptical — largely because of the romantic connection between Sarson's sister and Marshall — Wheaton kept on.

The turning point came on February 16, 1982, when he visited Maynard Chant at his home in Louisbourg.

Maynard, working in a fish plant, was now in his mid-twenties. His teen years of pushing street drugs and acting as a courier were now behind him. The fourteen-year-old who had skipped out of church back in 1971 was now twenty-four and had become a born-again Christian. His role in helping convict Donald Marshall now bothered him.

Harry Wheaton and another Mountie showed up at the fish plant and wanted to talk to him. For Maynard, it was a chance to clean the slate. He admitted he had lied in 1971. He said he was not even in the park when Seale was stabbed.

Aware now that he had an injustice on his hands, Wheaton broadened his search. John Pratico, too, was relieved to tell that he had lied at the trial. So did Patricia Harriss. Roy Ebsary was cautious, but eventually, on February 22, he phoned Wheaton and admitted to stabbing Seale. But when the Mounties tried to get an official statement, Ebsary refused.

Wheaton needed hard evidence.

Greg Ebsary, Roy's son, turned over ten knives that had been stored in a wooden basket in the Ebsary home. Analysis showed that one knife still held traces of fibres from the yellow jacket that Donald Marshall had worn that night almost eleven years earlier, and also fibres from the brown coat worn by Sandy Seale.

Now Wheaton had one last piece of the puzzle to gather. He still needed to talk to Donald Marshall Jr.

Wheaton's first visit with Marshall at Dorchester, on February 18, was cut short by a prison riot. But three weeks later, on March 9, 1982, two no-nonsense RCMP officers visited Donald Marshall Jr. at the penitentiary again.

Donald was ushered into an interview room: a small room two metres by two metres.

Donald was almost happy — and surprised — to see them. "So when do I get out?" he asked the two officers. It was a joke, but the fact that the RCMP were once again reviewing the case gave him hope.

"First you have to give us a story we can believe," said Staff Sergeant Harry Wheaton.

Donald couldn't believe his ears. Three weeks before, on February 18, he had repeated for these same two

RCMP officers his story of what happened that night ten-and-a-half years before.

"Whadda ya mean? I told you about Mitchell Sarson. He says Ebsary did it, just like I told you. Did you talk to him?"

Staff Sgt. Wheaton calmly took out his notebook.

"You see, Donald, it's this way. Mitchell's story is interesting. But we are having a hard time swallowing it. It's just another prison tale as far as we are concerned. I mean, come on. Mitchell's sister is your girlfriend."

"So?"

"Can't you see how that looks? Maybe there's Mitchell making up this story about Ebsary just so we can spring you from jail."

"It ain't like that."

"Okay, if it ain't like that, then tell us what really went down that night. As I said, give us a story we can believe."

"I did."

Wheaton sighed. "No, you didn't, Donald. Because we don't believe your story."

He sounded serious. Donald fought back his anger.

"But that sonnabitch did it. Everybody knows that but you guys."

Staff Sgt. Wheaton pointed to his notebook. "We need something we can take to court," he said. "You see,

Donald, we did talk to your girlfriend's brother. And then we did talk to Roy Ebsary."

Staff Sgt. Wheaton paused.

"Mr. Ebsary admits that he stabbed Sandy Seale."

The two men locked eyes. Silence filled the room. From further down the hall, someone slammed a door.

Donald felt an enormous load lift from his shoulders.

"Then I can get out of here?" he replied.

"It's not that simple, Donald. You see, Mr. Ebsary says that the stabbing happened when you and Sandy were trying to rob them. He's saying it was self-defence." It was a story that Wheaton found hard to believe, but he felt he needed to get Marshall's side of the story. It was the one weak spot in his investigation.

"Self-defence? That's a crock. He …"

"The thing is, he has a slightly different version of the events than you do. Now, if you were to tell us a story we could believe, if what you say lined up with what else we've heard, if you give us something we could take to court, this could end well."

"But I told you what happened."

Wheaton slowly closed his notebook and began to rise from his chair. "Or we could play it the other way. Do you really want us to walk away and never see you again? Do you want to rot in this hellhole?"

"But he says he did it? He admitted that to you?"

Both Staff Sgt. Wheaton and the other officer with him nodded.

"Now tell us what happened that night."

Donald crossed his arms. He wasn't sure what they wanted, but for the first time in eleven years he felt he might get out of prison. Years before, in order to win a transfer to Springhill, Donald had lied and said he had stabbed Sandy. What kind of story did they want this time? If it got him out of prison, he thought, he'd tell them almost anything.

Staff Sgt. Wheaton leaned forward, almost friendly. "So first: you'd said you went to Halifax that day?" he asked.

The other cop had his pen poised over his notebook.

"Yeah, with Roy Gould, Pauline Bernard. Some other woman."

"What time did you get back?"

"About nine-thirty p.m."

Halifax is about five hours by car from Sydney. On return from Halifax, Donald described a trip to a liquor store and a tavern. He left and walked through Wentworth Park, where he met Sandy.

"Where was he going?"

"I remember Sandy telling me he came from the dance and said he was heading home."

"Anybody else?"

"Bobby Patterson came down from behind the band-shell. He was very drunk."

"Did you talk to him?"

"I recall asking him if he knew us. He was also stoned on acid. He said he did. He was very drunk so we put him under some bushes so police wouldn't get him."

Staff Sgt. Wheaton looked at him without blinking. "But you weren't in the park just to be nice to people."

Donald shifted his gaze from one cop to another.

"I ... I asked Sandy if he wanted to make some money."

"And?"

"He asked how. I explained that we could roll someone."

"You've done that before." From Sgt. Wheaton, this was not a question.

"A few times."

"So that's when you started to look for someone to roll."

Donald continued, mixing his memory of what happened with the story the cops obviously wanted to hear. To him, "rolling" someone meant simply asking for loose change. Asking them to "roll" out their pockets. Not a legal activity, but closer to energetic panhandling than robbery.

"The first time I saw the two fellows we later decided to rob was on the George Street side of the park. The short, old guy I now know as Ebsary was dressed like he came off a boat. He had a blue coat over his shoulders."

"But you were on the other side of the park." Again, not a question.

"My memory is poor on how we got over to the Crescent Street side of the park," Donald said. To make his story believable, he had to blur the line between the truth and fabrication.

"Who else did you see?"

"I remember seeing Patricia Harriss and Terry Gushue and giving Terry a light. Sandy went over and talked to Ebsary and the other guy. The three of them would be maybe twenty yards from Patricia, Terry, and me."

"And then you joined them?"

"I then walked down Crescent Street to Sandy and the two guys."

"What did you talk about?"

"We talked about everything — women, booze, about them being priests, and hinted around about money. The two guys started to walk away from us, and I called them back. They then knew we meant business about robbing them." Donald wondered if they were believing the robbery thing.

"Tell me what happened."

"I got in a shoving match with the one guy. Sandy took the short, old guy. I don't remember exactly what was said, but I definitely remember Ebsary saying 'I got something for you' and then stabbing Sandy. I let go of the guy I had and Ebsary came at me.

"He swung the knife at me, and I held off the knife with my left hand. The knife sort of caught my jacket, and I pulled free and ran and felt blood running from the cut. I can't describe the knife, and Sandy fell and stayed there. I ran across the bridge and ran into Chant. I told him what happened."

The guy with the notebook looked up.

Staff Sgt. Wheaton shifted his bulk in his chair.

"That seems to fit better with what we know."

Donald leaned forward, his elbows on the table.

"I definitely did not stab Sandy Seale," he said. "I saw Ebsary do it."

Staff Sgt. Wheaton looked him in the eye. "Why didn't you tell that to the police at the time? You would have saved a lot of trouble."

"I told them. I ..."

"No. About the robbery."

Donald shifted in his chair. He was not comfortable. "I thought I would get into more trouble. I never told my lawyers or the Court. I just thought I would get in more trouble. I felt bad about Sandy dying, as it was my idea … to … rob these guys. I knew Sandy but not real well, and it's too bad he died. But I didn't kill him. Ebsary did it."

"Will you testify in court?"

"If Ebsary goes to court? You bet. I am willing to take a polygraph test to prove I am innocent. I did not stab Sandy. I gave the police a statement when it happened, and a week later I was picked up by MacIntyre. He didn't question me very much. He said he had two witnesses to say I did it and locked me up."

The officer with the notebook continued writing. Finally, he pushed his notebook across the table.

"I've taken down your statement," he said. "Read it over and then sign it." He indicated with his pen where the signature should go.

Donald read through the handwritten notes. The officers seemed to think the part about the robbery was good. Well, so did Donald, even if he had made it up. At that point he'd have said anything that would get him out of prison.

He signed the statement. Like much about this case, that simple action cost him dearly.

21

CHAPTER TWENTY-ONE

NO INJUSTICE HERE

For the first time in more than ten years, Donald began to feel some hope. Now someone else admitted to the stabbing. What more was needed to set him free?

It would not be so simple.

Shortly after signing that statement, Donald Marshall Jr. was released on parole and began working with the Department of Indian Affairs and Northern Development.

The RCMP investigation provided his lawyer with more than enough ammunition for another appeal. Three key witnesses — Patricia Harriss, Maynard Chant, and John Pratico — all retracted their testimonies. All told the Mounties the same story they had first told the Sydney police: they had not seen the stabbing.

Their stories also confirmed Donald's original version of events.

By June 1982, Donald had spent eleven years and thirty-one days in prison for a murder he did not commit. Then, the Honourable Jean Chrétien, Attorney General of Canada (later to become Prime Minister), ordered an appeal hearing.

Normally, once findings of facts have been made by a lower court, an appeal court considers only questions of law. But Donald's new lawyer, Stephen Aronson, argued successfully that circumstances were different.

He asked the court to deal not only with the law, but also in this case to consider new evidence "that bears upon a decisive or potentially decisive issue in the trial."

This new evidence, he argued, if it had been available at the original trial, "could reasonably when taken with other evidence adduced at trial, be expected to have affected the result." Translated from lawyer talk, this meant if these facts had been known in 1971, Donald would have been cleared — or perhaps there would have been no trial at all.

When he was released in April, Donald had been granted day parole.

After some months of legal to-and-fro, the court heard final arguments in February 1983. A decision was released on May 10 of that same year — eighteen days shy of twelve years after the stabbing in Wentworth Park.

The court concluded that in light of all the evidence before it, "no reasonable jury could, on that evidence, find Donald Marshall Jr. guilty of the murder of Sandy Seale."

"In such a case, a new trial should ordinarily be required ... However, no purpose would be served in so doing. The evidence now available, with the denials of Pratico and Chant that they saw anything, could not support a conviction of Marshall.

"Accordingly, we ... direct that a judgment of acquittal be entered in favour of the appellant.

"Donald Marshall Jr. was convicted of murder and served a lengthy period of incarceration. That conviction is now set aside."

Donald heard the news when he went to the Victoria General Hospital in Halifax to visit his ailing father. His mother met him with tears flowing. Donald feared something had happened to his father.

But his mother hugged him tightly. "The court says you're innocent," she said. "You are free!"

Arm in arm, they swept into the room where Donald Sr. was undergoing dialysis. The two men embraced. It was the moment Junior had dreamt of for almost twelve years.

Later, Donald would learn that the finding came with a nasty hook. No longer able to carry the financial strain of the unpaid legal bill, Stephen Aronson was quitting law. And through Aronson, Donald was told that the court left him with a parting shot that would haunt him and keep the issue before the public for another six years. The court had added:

"Any miscarriage of justice is, however, more apparent than real.

"In attempting to defend himself against the charge of murder, Mr. Marshall admittedly committed perjury for which he still could be charged …

"There can be no doubt but that Donald Marshall's untruthfulness through this whole affair contributed in large measure to his conviction.

"However, the fact remains that Marshall's new evidence, despite his evasions, prevarications, and outright lies, supports the evidence of James MacNeil's story."

In other words, Donald Marshall Jr. was not guilty, and his conviction had been caused by the lies of others, but the whole mess was still his own fault.

22

CHAPTER TWENTY-TWO

JUSTICE DENIED

In January 1990, Donald Marshall Jr. waited anxiously in the MicMac Native Friendship Centre in Halifax to avoid reporters.

For the past several years, he had been the centre of attention. It seemed that ever since he got out of prison, he had been in the middle of a storm.

For the past three years, his case had been the focus of a Royal Commission. Now, finally, the commission was about to release its findings.

His lawyer at the Royal Commission, Anne Derrick, (now a provincial court judge), said Donald waited anxiously "to hear what the Commission had to say about the wrongs perpetrated against him."

His experience did not give him much hope. Even when he was released from prison, the appeal court had said the whole mess was his fault.

"He had learned, through bitter, wrenching experience that he could not trust the justice system," Derrick
wrote twenty years later.

The years in prison, the slap in the face at his release,
had taken their toll. Now he was angry, discouraged, and
had a hard time trusting even those closest to him. He did
not hold out a lot of hope that the Royal Commission
would change anything.

In 1982 when he got out of prison, Donald thought
he was free. But the rebuke from the court — blaming
him for his own conviction — stung him. How, he asked
himself, was he to blame for the shoddy police work? For
the lying witnesses? For lawyers who didn't do all they
could?

To add to the humiliation, he had a legal bill of
almost $80,000 that he could not pay. His lawyer, Stephen
Aronson, had basically worked for free up to that point.
A beginning lawyer with a young family, Aronson had
sacrificed his beginning law practice and threw himself
into the Marshall case. The effect was traumatic: by the
time Donald was freed, Aronson suffered career burnout.
He quit law.

In comic books, being a hero seems easy. In real life,
it comes at a cost.

Shortly after Donald was released from prison,

Aronson introduced him to a reporter, Michael Harris. Harris, a Toronto native, worked for *The Globe and Mail*, a national newspaper.

Over the next four years, Harris interviewed Donald Marshall Jr. many times and spent hours with the young Mi'kmaq. At his original trial, Donald had been inarticulate and frightened. He had grown up. He had become more articulate, an angry man, who later would become what some described as a gifted speaker.

The hours of interviews with Marshall, along with the extensive transcripts of court hearings and trials, resulted in a book that shook the legal world in 1986: *Justice Denied: The Law Versus Donald Marshall*, by Michael Harris, published by Macmillan of Canada. The book told the story of Donald Marshall Jr. in painful and blunt detail.

The story was a stunning indictment of police, the courts, and lawyers. It got the attention it sought. It pulled no punches. It showed Donald as a rowdy, trouble-making teen who survived prison through physical strength and willpower.

But it also clearly depicted his mistreatment by the justice system. The book drew national attention. The country wanted to know: why did this go so wrong?

Embarrassed, the Government of Nova Scotia created

a Royal Commission to examine the investigation of the death of Sandy Seale as well as the prosecution and conviction of Donald Marshall Jr. for that murder.

A Royal Commission is a powerful tool for investigating corruption, crime, and government operation. The government defines the terms of reference. Once begun, even the government that created it cannot stop a Royal Commission.

The terms set for this Royal Commission were to:

"… make recommendations to the Governor in Council respecting the investigation of the death of Sandford William Seale on the 28-29th day of May A.D. 1971; the charging and prosecution of Donald Marshall, Jr. with that death; the subsequent conviction and sentencing of Donald Marshall Jr. for the non-capital murder of Sandford William Seale for which he was subsequently found to be not guilty; and such other related matters which the Commissioners consider relevant to the Inquiry."

Translation: to find out what happened.

Under Chief Justice T. Alexander Hickman of Newfoundland, the Commission began its work. It took three years plus a month. It cost more than seven million dollars. The seven-volume report included thousands of pages of extra material and documents.

At the end of it, upstairs in the Friendship Centre, Donald waited to hear the findings. His nervousness reached a peak as his lawyer, Anne Derrick, walked across the room towards him.

Donald looked up at her, not daring to ask.

But Derrick broke into a smile.

"Junior, you've been vindicated," she said. "The report says that the justice system failed you at virtually every turn."

Derrick describes this as a transformative moment. "For the first time since I met Junior, there was visible relief," she wrote in 2009. "It was as though something vast and heavy had been lifted off him."

The details of that Royal Commission report show this was no exaggeration. The report has been the foundation of facts for this book. As the reader may have gathered by now, the picture the report painted was not pretty.

Few of the people involved escaped blame.

The first police officer on the scene was Detective Michael Bernard MacDonald. He was the same officer who saw a blood-soaked, fourteen-year-old Maynard Chant as "a normal hitchhiker". The Commission said:

"This is no satisfactory excuse for MacDonald not taking formal statements from Marshall and Chant that night."

The Royal Commission said that police were incompetent for not securing the crime scene and taking no statements the night of the stabbing.

Sgt. of Detectives John MacIntyre (and later Police Chief) was called a liar who bullied the teenaged witnesses to change their stories. The Commission: "The use of tactics that a fourteen-year-old may reasonably consider intimidating is improper."

In 1987, the Commission asked MacIntyre: "Who do you believe stabbed Sandy Seale?" His answer: "I would leave that to the courts; although, I have my own problems with it." After sixteen years, he still could not admit he had made an error.

MacIntyre's assistant, Detective William Urquhart, "should have realized that MacIntyre was pursuing only his own theory of the stabbing. … In failing to speak up … Urquhart failed in his responsibilities as a police officer." Three years later, when Donna Ebsary told of seeing her father washing blood from a knife, Urquhart had been the one to investigate. "He had a duty to see that this new information was passed on to his superior. This he failed to do."

Crown Prosecutor Donald C. MacNeil, the

Commission said, had an interest "to see that justice was done." By not providing full disclosure of evidence to the defence, he failed in this duty.

Donald's two defence lawyers were also found wanting. Rosenblum was considered a skilled defence lawyer; Khattar had a long and distinguished career. Both were paid substantial fees and had access to funds needed to provide for Marshall's defence. But "They let him down," the Commission said. "We consider their actions, or lack thereof, to be the antitheses of what one would expect from competent, skilled counsel."

The trial judge, Mr. Justice Louis Dubinsky, made a number of incorrect rulings. The worst of these was not allowing defence to explore John Pratico's change in testimony. "We believe a full and complete cross-examination of John Pratico ... would have resulted in his recanting evidence. ... In those circumstances, no jury would have convicted Donald Marshall Jr."

The list of those who failed in basic duties continued long after Donald was convicted.

After Jimmy MacNeil approached Sydney police a week after Donald's conviction, the RCMP took over. Inspector Alan Marshall of the RCMP admitted to the Commission that he had "botched the investigation."

The court was not kind to him: "His lack of effort is

shocking. If he had done any real investigation, he would have discovered that Donald Marshall Jr. did not stab Sandy Seale. ... (his) incompetent investigation was a major contributing factor in Donald Marshall's spending eleven years in jail."

The Attorney General's department of the Nova Scotia government did not escape the wrath of the Commission. In the fall of 1971, the first appeal of the case began. Jimmy MacNeil had come forward by then — but no one told the defence lawyers.

Said the Commission:

"... the Department of Attorney General failed to ensure that all relevant issues were raised, and we believe that failure contributed to the denial of Marshall's appeal and to his continued incarceration."

If MacNeil's statement had been brought to the attention of defence counsel, "it is all but inevitable that a new trial would have been ordered."

Not even one of the heroes of the case, Staff Sgt. Harry Wheaton, escaped criticism. Although originally skeptical, Wheaton quickly began to believe Marshall was innocent. His investigation "formed the basis of the evidence that led to Marshall's acquittal."

However, Wheaton had pressured Marshall into making up a story about trying to rob Ebsary and

MacNeil. The Commission felt that the officers placed stress on Marshall by telling him they believed "there was something else going on in the park other than just a casual walk through the park to catch a bus" on the night Sandy Seale was killed.

"They simply should have asked Marshall to tell them the facts," the Commission ruled. The tale of robbery limited the compensation Donald received. (He received $270,000, out of which he had to pay his own legal costs of $100,000.)

Blaming Donald for the miscarriage was the final straw.

"We are at a loss," wrote the Commission, "to understand how the Court of Appeal could conclude that there was no miscarriage of justice when, on the evidence before it, Marshall's conviction was secured by perjured testimony obtained through police pressure, and his counsel were precluded from full cross-examination because of lack of disclosure by the Crown.

"For any citizen to spend eleven years in jail in a federal penitentiary for a crime he did not commit constitutes — even in the narrowest sense — a miscarriage of justice in the extreme."

Racist attitudes — and cultural assumptions — proved to be at the heart of the miscarriage. During the hearing itself, Donald Marshall Sr. took pains to explain what this might mean.

Chief Counsel for the Commission, George MacDonald, put it this way: "I came to appreciate the wisdom that Chief Marshall possessed," he wrote. "I came to understand that the Mi'kmaq can be very reserved people who react differently, for example, to aggressive questioning. Once Chief Marshall explained this to me, I noticed how potential Mi'kmaq witnesses ... had difficulty looking me in the eye."

"I learned a tremendous amount from this very accomplished man," the lawyer said.

The Commission produced a list of eighty-two recommendations that concerned minority and human rights, training of police and Crown attorneys, police procedures on dealing with underage witnesses, and the right of anyone charged with a crime to the right of full disclosure — that is, to all the details of the police investigation, even of witnesses not called.

Of the eighty-two recommendations, twenty-seven concerned the rights of natives and minorities.

The common thread through the whole story? Why did Donald Marshall Jr. suffer so at the hands of the justice system?

The Commission stated it frankly:

"One reason Donald Marshall Jr. was convicted of and spent eleven years in jail for a murder he did not commit is because Marshall is an Indian."

23

CHAPTER TWENTY-THREE

FISHING RIGHTS

When he was released from prison in 1982, Donald went fishing. He took a boat out into the Atlantic Ocean near Peggy's Cove and spent some time alone: just him, the sea, the sky, and rocking waves. He had come home.

Ten years later, Donald went fishing again.

This time his aim was to exercise the rights he felt he had as a native Canadian. Unfortunately, officials from the Department of Fisheries and Oceans had a problem with that. Three problems, actually.

Donald was fishing out of season.

His nets were illegal.

And he had no licence.

Told to stop, Donald — never one to feel authority was to be obeyed — kept fishing.

He called his friend, Mi'kmaq Chief Terrance Paul,

and asked for advice. "I told him to keep fishing," Chief Paul said.

So he did.

But when he came ashore and sold the catch of the day — some 210 kilograms of eels — his efforts earned $787.10. That's when the real trouble started.

Donald was charged with illegal fishing.

Thus began Donald's second major court battle. This one lasted six years, and put native fishermen against non-native fishermen, the government against native fishermen, and made headlines across the country.

Backed by native lawyers, Donald fought the charges all the way to the Supreme Court of Canada. His lawyers argued that historic treaty rights dating back to 1760 granted the Mi'kmaw people rights to fish for a living.

Six years later, in 1999, the Supreme Court handed down its decision: Donald Marshall Jr. had the legal right to fish for eels out of season. The Court agreed that the ancient treaty gave aboriginals the right to a "moderate livelihood" from fishing.

The results astonished all who watched — and the whole nation did.

Native fishermen added to their equipment, feeling that the court had granted them the right to fish as much as they wanted when they wanted. Non-native fishermen did not like that, claiming that natives should abide by the same laws as non-natives. In protest, non-native fisherman threatened natives, federal fisheries officials rammed native boats.

In an effort to calm the issue, the Supreme Court offered a "clarification" on the issue, often referred to as Marshall 2. It upheld the treaty rights, but also maintained that the federal government had the right to regulate native fishing for conservation.

The resulting conflicts saw one man beaten with a baseball bat, and shots fired from the bow of a fishing boat. Helicopters circled over native boats, and at one point the federal government destroyed more than 2,000 First Nations lobster traps. Lives were threatened, fisheries department boats rammed and sank native fishing boats, and native fishermen set up an armed camp to defend their rights. Some described it as a small war.

After he saw the violence that the court decision stirred up, Donald Marshall was shocked. "Everything is way out of control right now," he said. "I don't want anybody to get hurt. Our leaders, federal officials, and others have to sit down and work it out or all hell will break loose."

That didn't mean giving up. Donald joined peaceful protests urging native leaders not to give up the fight.

"We've got to keep fighting," he said. "It's not only me — I don't want our kids in another ten years fighting the same s---."

At the centre of this storm, Donald — the young man who had fought his way through the tough land of a federal penitentiary — asked for reason on both sides.

It took two years, but eventually the federal government compensated native fishermen for lost traps, and native fishermen were granted the right to fish for sustenance and ceremonial purposes but denied the right to fish commercially out of season.

In his first fight for his own justice, Donald Marshall Jr. changed the way aboriginal Canadians are treated in the courts, by police, by the government, and even how they assert their own rights.

In the battle over fishing rights, Donald Marshall Jr. once again changed the lot of aboriginal peoples in Canada.

24

CHAPTER TWENTY-FOUR

DONALD'S LEGACY

He was a rowdy teen, of that there are no doubts.

But conviction for a crime he did not commit scarred him for life.

In another time and place, Junior might have been a movie star. His good looks and athletic body were right for that role. Although by nature a soft-spoken, gentle man, in later life some described him as a "gifted" speaker.

Tall and fit, he might have been a professional athlete. Anyone tough enough to break his wrist in a prison fist-fight could protect himself anywhere.

He was expelled from school at the age of fifteen while in the seventh grade. Armed with little more than a grade-six education, upgraded to grade ten along with trade certificates earned while in prison, he forever changed the laws of Canada — twice. As noted in the previous chapter, the first time was for himself; the second time was for his people.

What might he have accomplished had he not been unjustly convicted?

Perhaps in his twenties, his wild teen years behind him, he might have grown into responsibility and leadership. He had much to offer.

Instead, when he was released from prison in his late twenties, he carried mental and physical scars. Survival in prison meant fights. Loneliness and depression often followed.

Throughout the rest of his life, his anger would break through at unpredictable times. This anger was often fueled by drugs and alcohol — addictions that he broke free from eventually. At such times, it was the people closest to him who suffered the most.

Acting like a seventeen-year-old is normal — for someone who is seventeen. Donald had left school in the seventh grade and spent most of his teen years socialized in the Shipyard Gang. The skills learned in a teen gang and in prison are not very useful in the adult world.

Even in the decade before he died, he faced personal legal challenges. He was charged with attempted murder. He was accused of trying to run over another man with a vehicle. The charges were later dropped when Donald and the victim took part in a healing circle. In 2004, he faced charges of spousal abuse and threatening his wife, non-native, Colleen D'Orsay.

But his legacy to his native Canadians, and to the Membertou people, is more solid.

From 1927 until 1951, the Indian Act made it illegal for First Nations to hire a lawyer or raise money to begin legal proceedings against the government. The Marshall case on the fishing treaty right was the first time that the Mi'kmaq in Nova Scotia acted to engage in legal action to uphold treaty rights.

The Royal Commission forced a province and a nation to face up to the reality of racial discrimination. Because of Donald Marshall Jr., the justice system in Nova Scotia has changed radically. Dr. Daniel Paul told me in an email exchange that minorities are no longer blatantly discriminated against in the court system. Police forces and the training of police officers have changed.

Racism still exists, but compared to what existed forty years ago it is miniscule. There is, however, still much to do. As of 2009, Nova Scotia had only one African Canadian serving as a judge — and no one from Mi'kmaw nation.

"All minorities in the province and the country owe him a great deal," Dr. Paul said. "The tenacity shown by him and his father in proclaiming his innocence, and proving it, has made Nova Scotia and Canada a better place for us all to reside in!"

Much of the discrimination in this case came from poverty. Not family poverty, though even with both parents working, the large family could never be described as rich. Sydney in the 1950s and 1960s was impoverished. Donald's rowdy teen years were the result of a time and place.

Today, the economy of the Membertou Nation has also improved significantly. The initiatives of the Membertou Nation provide employment for many non-natives in the Sydney area. Native leaders are now invited to participate in boards and commissions — and more important, are listened to.

As well, the Donald Marshall Junior Memorial Award honours his courage in the legal battle to free himself of a racially motivated wrongful murder conviction and for his contribution towards recognition of Aboriginal treaty rights. The award is presented annually at the Dalhousie Schulich School of Law to a third-year graduating student who raises awareness of legal issues affecting Aboriginal peoples.

He became a hero to his people and was admired by people in all walks of life.

In the 1990s, Donald ran camps for at-risk aboriginal youth until his health deteriorated.

In 2003, he underwent a double-lung transplant. His health never fully recovered. Anti-rejection drugs were blamed when he died in 2009 at the age of fifty-five.

The community has honoured both Donald and his father. In 2010, statues of both were unveiled to greet visitors to the Membertou Trade & Convention Centre.

Wela'lin Junior. We wish you peace. M'sit Nokamaq.

"We're happy that he's at peace now."
    — Donald's brother, David, August 6, 2009

WHERE ARE THEY NOW?

DONALD MARSHALL JR. died August 6, 2009, from complications of a double-lung transplant. He was fifty-five.

DONALD MARSHALL SR. died in 1991. In 2010, Donald Sr. and Donald Jr. were each honoured by the Membertou Nation with statues that greet visitors to the Membertou Trade & Convention Centre in Sydney, Nova Scotia.

JOHN MACINTYRE retired as chief of police in Sydney in 1985 at the age of sixty-five. He died September 30, 2009, at the age of ninety — fifty-five days after the death of Donald Marshall Jr.

JIMMY MACNEIL continued to live in Whitney Pier, Sydney, for twenty or more years. The data and circumstances of his death could not be confirmed.

MAYNARD CHANT became a born-again Christian and for a time joined his father in the family funeral-home business. He still lives in Cape Breton.

JOHN PRATICO testified at the Royal Commission hearing that completely exonerated Donald Marshall Jr. He admitted lying at the original trial by saying that he had seen the stabbing, and received an ovation from the courtroom spectators. His current whereabouts is not known.

PATRICIA HARRISS also recanted her testimony given at the original trial and told the 1989 Royal Commission she had been coerced by police. Her present location is not known.

HARRY WHEATON returned to uniform duty after performing the second RCMP re-investigation of the Marshall case. His present location is unknown.

DONNA EBSARY returned from the U.S. to tell the Royal Commission that she had witnessed her father, Roy Ebsary, wash blood from a knife the night Sandy Seale was stabbed. Her current location is unknown.

ROY EBSARY was convicted in 1985 on his third trial for the stabbing of Sandy Seale. On appeal, his three-year sentence was reduced to one year in county jail. He died in 1988 in a Sydney boarding house. He was seventy-five.

AUTHOR'S NOTE

In the beginning of this book, I quoted from the Royal Commission that said Donald Marshall Jr. was convicted because he was a Native person. The racism was systemic; almost everyone who touched the case is blamed. But I also think it is important to credit those who were instrumental in righting this wrong.

In my earlier book in this series on the Steven Truscott case in Ontario, I pointed out that Steven was eventually cleared because of the work of two journalists and a lawyer.

Similarly, Donald Marshall Jr. was cleared and finally exonerated because of the work of three people — two lawyers and a journalist:

• Stephen Aronson, the young lawyer who worked tirelessly on the case almost without pay and successfully earned an appeal and acquittal for Donald.

• Journalist Michael Harris, whose book, *Justice Denied*, was instrumental in the formation of the Royal Commission into the Marshall prosecution.

• Judge Ann Derrick of the Provincial Court of Nova Scotia. As a lawyer, she represented Donald at the Royal Commission hearing and was the one who delivered to Donald the news of his complete exoneration.

These three demonstrate the best that lawyers and journalists can be.

GLOSSARY

ACQUITTAL: the verdict when someone accused of a crime is found not guilty.

APPEAL: a request to review a case that has already been decided in court. An appeal must be based on points of law or, in rare cases, a change in evidence or testimony.

ASSAILANT: a person accused of beating up or attacking another person.

BARRISTER: a lawyer. Someone educated in law and representing a person.

BOOTLEGGER: someone who sells liquor illegally.

CONVICTION: the verdict when someone accused of a crime is found guilty.

COUNSEL: lawyer.

CROSS-EXAMINATION: After a witness for either the defence or for the Crown tells what he or she knows, a lawyer for the other side gets to ask questions of the witness.

CROWN ATTORNEY: the lawyer(s) acting for the government, or "the Crown," in court proceedings. They are the prosecutors in Canada's legal system. Sometimes called Crown Counsel.

DEFENDANT: the person who has been formally accused of and charged with committing a crime.

DIALYSIS: a medical procedure to clear urine from the blood when kidneys have failed.

EXONERATED: found to be free of blame.

FABRICATION: made up; lies.

FULL DISCLOSURE: revealing important or requested evidence to the other side in a trial. In 1991 (largely due to the Donald Marshall Jr. case) the Supreme Court of Canada ruled that the Crown had a duty to reveal its evidence to the defence before a trial. Before 1991, disclosure was voluntary.

INDICTMENT: a formal charge against an individual

JURY: A criminal trial is decided by a group of twelve randomly-selected citizens from the province in which the trial is held. All twelve must agree on a verdict.

MINORITY: a small part of a whole. In society, persons of a race who are not the same as most others. If those persons have racial features they are often referred to as visible minorities.

PAROLE: release from prison before the full sentence has been served. A prisoner on parole must agree to certain restrictions and report regularly to a parole officer.

PEERS: people of a similar legal status.

PENITENTIARY: a prison for serving sentences of

more than two years. Maximum security prisons (like Dorchester, N.B.) operate under heavy security. Minimum security prisons allow more freedom for prisoners.

PERJURY: lying in a court of law. It is a crime.

PERPETRATOR: someone guilty of an act.

PRELIMINARY HEARING: a hearing held to decide if there is enough evidence for a trial. This is held after the accused has been charged with a crime.

PROBATION: a sentence imposed often on young offenders in place of prison or jail.

PROSECUTOR: the lawyer acting for the prosecution, usually the state (in Canada, the Crown). The prosecutor tries to prove the defendant is guilty.

RACIALIZED: having to do with the race of people involved. Donald Marshall, Jr. was treated badly in part because of his race.

RACISM: having to do with race, usually in a negative way.

REP HOCKEY: a hockey team representing players from a given area. Usually, in house league hockey, everyone who joins gets to play. Rep (or representative) hockey players must try out to make a team, and the team will represent the area or city against other similar teams.

RESERVE: land set aside for the use of Indian bands or tribes.

RULING: a decision made by a judge during a court hearing.

(SIC): so it is in the original. In a quoted passage, this indicates a word is used as it appears in the source.

TESTIMONY: the statement of a witness under oath.

TRANSCRIPTS: word-for-word written reports of a trial.

VERDICT: the decision of the jury at the end of a trial, usually guilty or not guilty.

FURTHER READING

Justice Denied: The Law Versus Donald Marshall by Michael Harris (Macmillan of Canada, Toronto, 1986). The book is available through most used book sales outlets and in some libraries.

Justice Denied (movie): Based on the true story of this tragic and controversial case as recorded in the best-selling book by Michael Harris, *Justice Denied* is a searing indictment of "white man's justice" that traces the dramatic events leading to Marshall's arrest, trial, and nightmarish prison ordeal. (Directed by Paul Cowan. National Film Board of Canada, 1989.)

ADVANCED READING
Royal Commission on the Donald Marshall Jr., Prosecution. The full report consists of seven volumes. The core deliberations of the Royal Commission are in Volume 1 and served as the major source of information for this book. KEN7970.A74 A15 1989.

WEBSITES

Dr. Daniel Paul's website:
www.danielnpaul.com/DonaldMarshallJr.-1971.html

Membertou website:
www.membertou.ca/main-page.asp

PHOTO GALLERY:
Unveiling of statue for Donald Marshall Sr.
www.membertou.ca/view-gallery.asp?id=18

Unveiling of statue for Donald Marshall Jr.
www.membertou.ca/view-gallery.asp?id=21

Additional resources, including statements of some witnesses, are available on the author's website:
www.billswan.ca

With thanks to Dr. Daniel Paul and his helpful website; and to the library at Durham College/UOIT for providing a copy of the Royal Commission on the Prosecution of Donald Marshall, Jr. without which this book would not be possible.

INDEX